D1399381

Journeying
with
Julian

To Polly,

with fondest personal regards,

Hugh Hildersley +

St. Julian's Church, Norwich

The original church, which was subsequently destroyed
by bombing in the Second World War.

Illustration from M.M. Blake, *The Glory and Sorrow of Norwich,* 1898.

Journeying
with
Julian

C. Hugh Hildesley

MOREHOUSE PUBLISHING
Harrisburg, PA

This book is published in association with
the K. S. Giniger Company, Inc.

©1993 by C. Hugh Hildesley

Morehouse Publishing
P.O. Box 1321
Harrisburg, PA 17105

All rights reserved. No part of this book may be reproduced or transmitted
in any form or by any means, electronic or mechanical, including photo-
copying, recording, or by any information storage and retrieval system,
without written permission from the publisher.

Library of Congress Cataloging-in-Publication Data:
Hildesley, C. Hugh.
    Journeying with Julian / C. Hugh Hildesley.
       p.   cm.
    Includes bibliographical references.
    ISBN 0-8192-1594-5
       1. Julian of Norwich, b. 1343. 2. Mystics—England—
Biography.   3. Mysticism—England—History—Middle Ages, 600-1500.
4. Devotional literature, English (Middle)—History and criticism.
I. Title.
BV5095.J84H55   1993   93-23830
248.2'2'092—dc20   CIP

Printed in the United States of America by:
BSC LITHO
Harrisburg, PA 17105

Contents

Acknowledgments

Excerpts reprinted from *Julian of Norwich: Showings*, trans. by Edmund Colledge, O.S.A. and James Walsh, S.J. © 1978 by The Missionary Society of St. Paul the Apostle in the State of New York, by permission of Paulist Press.

Quotations, and the Horarium of the Anchoress, reprinted from *Ancrene Riwle: Introduction and Part I, Studies Vol. 31*, by R.W. Ackerman and R. Dahood, © 1984, the Center for Medieval and Renaissance Studies, State University of New York at Binghamton. Used by permission.

Quotations from *Church and Society in Late Medieval England*, by R.N. Swanson, © 1989, Basil Blackwell, Oxford, England. Used by permission.

Quotations from *Love Was His Meaning, The Theology and Mysticism of Julian of Norwich*, by B. Pelphrey, © 1982, used by permission of the Institut fur Anglistik und Amerikanistik, University of Salzburg.

Quotations from *Julian of Norwich* by Grace Jantzen, © 1987, The Society for Promoting Christian Knowledge. Used by permission.

Quotation from *Conjectures of a Guilty Bystander* by Thomas Merton © 1965. Used by permission of Doubleday.

Map of Norwich (*Recluses in Medieval Norwich*) on page 26 prepared by Ian Dunn and Helen Sutermeister for the exhibition "Julian and Her Norwich" held in Norwich in 1973. Used by kind permission of Ian Dunn.

Abbreviations

CW   Edmund Colledge, O.S.A., and James Walsh, S.J. *Julian of Norwich, Showings,* New York: Paulist Press, 1978.

ET   Edmund Colledge, O.S.A., and James Walsh, S.J. *A Book of Showings to the Anchoress Julian of Norwich* 2 vols. Toronto: Pontifical Institute of Mediaeval Studies, 1978.

Preface

On May 8, 1373, a woman in the middle of her thirty-first year fell dangerously ill and was close to death. A priest was called to administer the last rites to her and her mother closed her eyelids, believing her to be at the point of death. At this time she received a series of visions which involved her personal identification with the crucified Christ. Upon her unexpected recovery, she wrote down a brief account of these visions, referring to them as "showings," and this account forms the text of what is known as the *Short Version of the Revelations of Divine Love* by Dame Julian, or Mother Julian, or Julian of Norwich, whom I shall simply call Julian in the context of this work. Julian has frequently been referred to as "St. Julian." In spite of her saintly character, she has, in fact, never been canonized. She took her name, Julian, from the parish church to which she was attached as an anchoress, St. Julian's of Conesford, which had been consecrated before the Conquest (A.D.1066) and which was probably dedicated to St. Julian of Antioch, monk and confessor, who is thought to have suffered martyrdom in A.D.358. Following twenty years of meditation upon her visions, Julian prepared a long version of the *Revelations*, and it is this longer text that has been the subject of my own contemplation. Neither text is known in its original manuscript, and we are therefore working with later transcriptions, which may well have come from a work that Julian dictated to a scribe. It is conceivable that she wrote the original in her own hand, but of this there is no evidence. What we are left with is the earliest surviving work in the English language by a woman. It is my purpose to share her spiritual journey with you, the reader, in a personal account of her times and her theology, and to apply what she has to say to us to the challenges and opportunities the church faces at the end of this twentieth century. Julian's theology is intensely personal, and this book contains much that is personal to my own theological understanding.

One of the principal insights I have gained from my study of Julian's *Revelations* is that, for her, being a Christian is a matter of being in a completely ongoing relationship with the Trinity, and that this relationship is particularly nurtured through our relationship to Christ. Everything is seen and done in the light of our being "oned" to Christ. How we pray; how we relate to one another; the choices we make in our lives—all these concerns can be satisfactorily undertaken only through our identification with Christ. The purpose of this book is to share with you how we might apply Julian's theology to the task of identifying ourselves with Christ in our complicated lives, since her message is timeless and God's purpose for us has not changed.

To carry out this purpose, I will first give a broad description of England as it was in the middle of the fourteenth century, and follow with a closer look at the Norwich in which Julian lived. I will then define Julian's theology, before examining the meaning of Julian's theology for today's church.

If you were hoping for a strictly scholarly and academic treatment of the subject, I would have to suggest that there are far better sources for you to consult. The limited amount of original material available has led to exhaustive studies by those who specialize in particular disciplines and fields of inquiry. Edmund Colledge, O.S.A., and James Walsh, S.J., have written the definitive work of textual criticism. Norman P. Tanner has published a remarkable study of the church in late medieval Norwich between 1370 and 1532, based on his detailed examination of surviving wills from Norwich in this period. The theology of Julian has been analyzed meticulously by Brant Pelphrey in *Love Was His Meaning: The Theology and Mysticism of Julian of Norwich.* Grace Jantzen's *Julian of Norwich* is an essential book for those who wish to explore both Julian's theology and her role as a female mystic in the tradition of Anglican spirituality. These works, along with others, are included in a bibliography at the end of this book, allowing further opportunities for acquaintanceship with the full range of Julian's contribution to our faith and our literary inheritance.

Julian's *Revelations* come to us in later medieval English. For those of us who have battled with Chaucer's *Prologue* at school, this language will be familiar. It could be said that Julian's language is Chaucerian English, though an argument could be advanced that it would be just as appropriate to state that Chaucer's language is Julian English. In either case, we are faced with a language of great poetic beauty, which was in transition toward the English we know and use today. However, the very similarity of this language to our own creates one of its greatest difficulties, since many of those words with which we are familiar have changed their precise meaning over the intervening six centuries and many of the words Julian used are not familiar to us at all today. While I strongly urge the reader to sample the *Revelations* in its original tongue, for the purposes of clarity I have made what for me turned out to be a difficult but practical choice of using the highly accurate translation into modern English of Edmund Colledge and James Walsh for the frequent quotations from the *Revelations* in this book. I have assuaged my conscience by also offering references to their critical edition of the original text with each quoted passage.

Much has been made of Julian's oft-quoted disclaimer that her revelations were made to "a simple unlettered creature" (CW, p.177; ET, p.285). I will be addressing the issue of Julian's education and literary sources in the body of this study, but it should be recognized that while Julian may have lacked a formal education in the classics—it would not have been available to a woman in her age—it is abundantly clear from her work that she was both widely read and theologically sophisticated in a manner that is still encountered in some of those who have read for orders in this day, rather than studying through formal affiliation with an university or seminary. Since Julian's experience reflects my own, I emphasize this to prevent the promulgation of the myth that Julian was merely a divinely inspired functional illiterate. Her absence of formal academic credentials in her day must surely have helped her to grasp the essence of the Christian message as we find it in the Gospels and as it was lived out by those first apostles and the leaders of the early church. It was her strong understanding of this essence of Christianity that attracted me to Julian's thinking from my first encounter with it.

As I became more familiar with the contents of the *Revelations*, I found myself continually sensing that Julian had simply stated a profound truth concerning the Christian faith in a way that was immediately intelligible to me. I kept saying to myself, "That's it! That's precisely the point! Now I understand!"

I believe that the reason for my reaction to Julian's theology is that at base it is highly orthodox. She was possibly a lone voice in her times, and much of her theology is at variance with the accepted beliefs of the church in her day, but her independence and theological rigor sprang from her being in touch with an eternal truth, which she had encountered outside the normative channels of the institutional church. As Julian herself points out, the church survives in spite of what we do to it. The church in the fourteenth and fifteenth centuries was a far cry from its origins and much in need of the reformation it was soon to experience. The evidence concerning the state of the church in Norwich, however, demonstrates that it was far from being in a state of total corruption, decay, and decline in the second half of the fourteenth century, thereby requiring the Reformation to correct its nefarious ways. Here the church actually flourished, although it had in its dogma developed some tenets of belief that neither Julian nor we would find acceptable. Julian retained complete loyalty to her "Mother Church" even as she attempted to recall it to its earlier and purer state of existence. Throughout her work she commends such loyalty. Thus, in proposing ways in which her thought might help us in examining the church today, I believe we should be guided by Julian to a sense of renewal from within rather than replacement or separatism. She did not suggest or encourage the formation of a "new" church.

Perhaps, then, Julian could best be described as a "radical traditionalist," offering new insights and methods of application to the earliest and most essential principles of our Christian belief. In this way, Julian's message is not subject to the restrictions of time and history. The timelessness of her theology reflects the timelessness of God's loving purpose. Divine love is the meaning of the *Revelations*. As Julian states it, "Love was his meaning" (CW, p.342; ET, p.733). God's love for us is always the meaning. Our response to this love, with love, is our purpose in life. It is my belief that this loving response can transform today's world and that such transformation is the principal priority for the church. To state it another way: If we can, with Julian, become sufficiently identified with Christ, then our every thought, statement, and action will be conditioned by our response to the question, "What would Christ have thought, said, or done in this situation?" The answers to that question will reflect the extent of our permeation in God's love.

PART I
JULIAN'S WORLD

Glasgow
Edinburgh
Carlisle
Durham
York
Bangor St. Asaph
Lincoln
Lichfield
Coventry
Walsingham
Kings Lynn
Great Yarmouth
Worcester
Ely
NORWICH
St. Davids
Bury St. Edmund's
Llandaff Hereford
Oxford
Cambridge
Bristol
Bath
LONDON
Wells
Rochester
Winchester
Exeter
Salisbury
Canterbury
Southampton
Melcombe Regis
Chichester
Weymouth

MAJOR CITIES AND CATHEDRAL CITIES IN FOURTEENTH CENTURY ENGLAND

1

England in the Mid-Fourteenth Century

The One Hundred Years War

Although England was more or less continually at war from 1290 onward, the One Hundred Years War is a misnomer for two possible reasons. First, it lasted well over one hundred years, ending in the Treaty of Troyes in 1420. Second, there were periods of peace and absence of military activity, during the reigns of monarchs of less belligerent mien, following serious attempts at peace, as in the Treaty of Calais in October 1360 and the Anglo-French Treaty of 1396.

War in this period took two forms, war abroad with foreign powers and war at home between rival factions for the crown. The fourteenth century was a period in which monarchy was beginning to come into its own as a concept. However, government was not yet fully centralized, and questions of succession created opportunities for internal strife which were to preoccupy monarchs for some time to come, possibly reaching their zenith with the well-known problems that confronted Henry VIII. The war abroad centered on the territorial and sovereign claims of France and England, principally as they related to Gascony. The Treaty of Paris in 1259 gave the French king rights of suzerainty over a vassal, in this case a sovereign of another nation. By 1303, when Edward I and Philip IV had reached an agreement in spite of this paradoxical complication, they in fact set the stage for what was to become an almost interminable struggle. The Plantagenets had no intention of giving up their enormous revenues from Gascony. War proved an expensive way to pursue their claims for both Edward I and Edward II, the latter of whom was averse to war and already sufficiently challenged in his strife with Scotland. Edward III, however, saw the need for strong military leadership, and his succession to the throne in 1327 boosted England's potential military fortunes. In October 1337, Edward laid his claim to the French crown. The organized campaign began two years later, in 1339. In this period the king would have raised his army using the feudal principle that his lords were responsible for supplying him with any troops necessary to defend the realm, at the lords' expense. Already this system was encountering some practical modification. The lords were permitted to send the king money in place of their own service and the supply of their troops. This system filtered down to those who could afford to pay their way to their local lord to avoid conscription. Thus the mercenary soldier became a reality during the One Hundred Years War. Victories at Crecy in 1346, the taking of Calais in 1347, and the victory at Poitiers in 1356 assured Edward III of popularity, but at vast economic cost. During the 1370s England's fortunes in war declined without any satisfactory conclusion to the hostilities. Richard II, succeeding to the throne in 1377, achieved no victories to compare with his predecessor's and the Treaty of 1396, taking place three years before the end of his reign, did not secure a lasting peace. Owen Glyndwr's Welsh rebellion kept Henry IV preoccupied from 1400 until 1410, with war continuing on the Continent, and it was his successor, Henry V, who was able to revive England's fortunes against the French with his famous victory at Agincourt in 1415 and his conquest of Normandy in 1419 and 1420. The strength of the monarchy in England and the king's ability to afford these prolonged periods of expensive warfare were considerably enhanced by the merging of the estates of the House of Lancaster with those of the crown by Henry IV in 1399, the principality of Wales having already been acquired by Edward I. It was, then, as a supremely powerful landholder that the monarch commanded both the service and the respect of a large proportion of his subjects.

England was thus technically at war throughout Julian's life. However, it would be a mistake to imagine this state of war from a twentieth century perspective. With the two World Wars still fresh in our memory, we tend to see the state of war as embracing all areas of existence. This was not so in the fourteenth century. There is ample evidence that for many it was business as usual. Trade and industry continued uninterrupted and fortunes were acquired in spite of the economic effects of a war, which in those days would have been fought on a much smaller human scale than that to which we have become accustomed.

The Black Death

In the spring of 1348, England was a thriving nation. With the victories at Crecy and Neville's Cross in 1346 and the capture of Calais in 1347, the war was going well. Trade with the Continent flourished, but it was as a result of this trade that England was to suffer an event which was to transform its history for the rest of the fourteenth century. In June or July of 1348, a ship put in to Melcombe Regis harbor, which now forms part of the town of Weymouth in Dorset, and from the vessel disembarked an unofficial passenger in the form of a rat that carried fleas infected with the bubonic type of plague, known in those days as "the pestilence", later to be christened the "Black Death", to distinguish it from later outbreaks of similar plagues. The *Grey Friars Chronicle* is responsible for the identification of the port of entry and, lest Melcombe be assigned too heavy a portion of the blame, it is equally possible that the plague gained entry at about the same time through other ports, such as Bristol and Southampton. The plague was rife on the Continent, and from our point of view it is interesting to note that in spite of the fact that Norwich was, after London, the leading trader with Europe, the disease did not enter Norwich through any foreign vessel but came across England via London, having arrived in East Anglia in March of 1349.

The plague that came to be known as the Black Death was indeed carried by fleas, often themselves passengers on rats, and occurred in three forms. The bubonic form was so named for the "buboes" or swellings that appeared in the groin and the armpit primarily, although other locations were recorded. Death usually took place within four or five days of the appearance of the first bubo. A more violent infection was the primary or pulmonary manifestation, which gave the sufferer an average of 1.8 days until death. The most violent form of the plague was the septicemic variety, wherein the insect-borne infection entered the bloodstream; in this variant, death followed within a matter of hours. Within a year, between a third and a half of the English population had succumbed to this disease, which struck with a speed that allowed it to eliminate whole village populations within the course of a week. For reasons that will become obvious, towns were much more seriously affected than rural areas, though few sections of the country proved immune to the devastation of this pandemic.

Norwich lost up to half of its total population and at least half of its clergy, who, in ministering to the sick and dying, were exposed more readily than the laity, many of whom sought relief from the plague by moving out of the infested city. The population of Norwich in the middle of the fourteenth century, a period in which the accuracy of any census must be viewed with a degree of skepticism, was in the region of 13,000. Allowing for what appears to have been an error in transcription, Blomefield's history suggests a death toll in Norwich of some five thousand souls, which later studies suggest as being remarkably accurate.

To understand the widespread effects of this disease, one needs to be familiar with the conditions that prevailed in urban areas at the time. Disease control and hygiene as community responsibilities were either in their infancy or unknown. Overcrowding of houses and populations was rampant. In the case of Norwich, such overcrowding would have been encouraged by the encasement of the whole city within its magnificent city walls, whose protection citizens would have enjoyed in spite of their close quarters. In many instances, especially in rural areas, animals were sheltered under the same roof as human beings, the byre abutting the living quarters. This presented an admirable opportunity for fleas to transfer their allegiance from animal to human being. The humans often slept many to one bed and were not given to the regular and frequent bathing with which we are familiar today. Clothing was worn until it became unserviceable and, although laundering took place, the general level of cleanliness was low. Such were the conditions in the homes, there was little possibility of isolating any who became sick, and any knowledge of the transmission of infection was rudimentary. The bulk of the population struggled to survive on a poor diet and in conditions of inadequate sanitation. Dysentry and diarrhea were common and weakened resistance to the plague. The overwhelming dirt, coupled with the warmth generated in the small, closely spaced dwellings, provided an ideal environment for the rat. As Philip Ziegler states the situation in his detailed account of the Black Death:

"The medieval house might have been built to specifications approved by a rodent council as eminently suitable for the rat's enjoyment of a healthy and carefree life" (Ziegler, 1969, p.157).

The narrow streets, which were scarcely more than open drainage channels, the excrement dumped from the windows, the dead animals left to rot in the streets, the lack of any organized street cleaning or emptying of cesspools—all contributed to the lightning speed with which the plague ran its course. London was not to experience its first formal garbage collection until the year 1400, and it is to be remembered that all of this was taking place three hundred years before the Great Plague of London.

Thus Norwich was literally decimated by this visitation, taking into account two further outbreaks in 1361-62 and 1369. The effect on the parishes of Norwich can be gauged by the fact that Episcopal institutions of clergy into "livings" (that is, parishes) went from an annual figure of 81 between March 1348 and March 1349, to an annual figure of 831 between March 1349 and March 1350. In many cases, parishes had a multiple number of institutions during this second period as one incumbent speedily followed another to the grave.

It has been generally assumed that the Black Death was the prime offender in the depopulation of Norfolk villages in the fourteenth century. This does not appear to be the case, since records indicate that Ringstead Parva alone ceased to exist between 1348 and 1351. The causes of depopulation had much more to do with the growth of employment in the cities, the changing nature of the agrarian economy (which was becoming less labor intensive), and the consequent shift of population to the urban areas.

Julian was to receive her visions only four years after the third outbreak of the plague in Norwich. Her confrontation with mortality, her appreciation for life, and her optimism in the face of her survival of both the plague and her own sickness, whatever form it took, infuse her whole account. The citizens of Norwich of her day were acutely conscious of the transience and uncertainty of life.

The Peasants' Rebellion

The Peasants' Rebellion of 1381 was the result of a compilation of circumstances that compounded the dissatisfaction of a large segment of the working poor. The final blow was the imposition of the poll tax in 1380, but it is necessary to go back to the midcentury to understand the roots of this movement.

The Black Death in 1348–49 and its return in 1361-62 and 1369 did much to reduce the number of available workers. Responding to the laws of supply and demand, falling prices put pressure on landlords. They were experiencing difficulty selling their crops, which had been tended by laborers who were demanding higher wages. The agricultural situation was rendered worse by serious cattle murrains in 1348, 1363, and 1369.

In an attempt to control the situation, a Statute of 1351, shortly after the first outbreak of the plague, pegged wages at the pre-Black Death level and made it illegal for workmen to leave their employment. Landlords also resorted to leasing their lands, placing the burden of earning a living on their tenant farmers and reaping the more secure income from the leaseholds. The medieval concept of serfdom was already being questioned when these circumstances gave the workers a power to negotiate that they had not previously enjoyed.

The poll tax, then as in Britain today, provided a convenient cause around which the dissatisfied could coalesce. In 1377 a poll tax of four pence was levied. In 1379 this was increased through a graduated poll tax according to means. In 1380 a new, ungraduated poll tax of one shilling (twelve pence) was instituted. This was grossly inequitable, placing pressure on the already struggling poor. Attempts at rigorous collection fanned the flames of resentment. The census underwent a rapid decline, reflecting not so much a real decline in population but rather a determination to evade the punitive demands of the new tax. To place these figures in perspective, a laborer's wage of six pence per day translates into an annual wage of nine pounds sterling. In 1370 a trained thatcher would earn just over four pence a day, his assistant only two pence per day. Thus a poll tax of one shilling (twelve pence) would be the equivalent of two days' pay, a serious incursion upon a subsistence-level wage.

Evasion alone proved insufficient remedy for the oppressed, and in June of 1381 a movement of resistance began to grow. The source of the rebellion was East Norfolk, and on June 14, 1381, a rabble began to form. Leaderless at first and sporadic in its actions, the movement soon attracted its leadership. Headed by one Geoffrey Litster, on June 17 a great band of rebels came together on Mousehold Heath and marched on the city of Norwich, demanding that the authorities open the city gates. Having gained entrance to the city, Litster established his headquarters in the castle in the center of the city and held a "state banquet," at which he was waited on by captive knights. A bill for a large quantity of wine survives, evidence that the company at least drank well! The mob plundered the city, among other acts removing and destroying by burning the rolls of the leaseholds of the Carrow Priory nunnery. The purpose of this record burning was, of course, to make the application of the poll tax impossible. In addition, the mob took the law into its own hands, conducting mock trials and executing those whom it chose to prosecute. Elsewhere John Ball, the preacher, was inciting the mobs to further rebellion, and Wat Tyler emerged as the overall leader of a group that decided to take its cause to London. Tyler was captured and executed. Litster, upon learning of this reversal, determined to send an embassy to London to seek an official pardon, armed with a considerable sum of money that had been levied on the citizens of Norwich. It is interesting to note that the embassy consisted of five persons of whom two, Sir William Morley and Sir John Brewer, were knights and three were peasants. This group was intercepted on June 24, at Newmarket by the Bishop of Norwich, Henry Despenser, who then returned with his captives to Norwich, having engaged the rabble in battle at North Walsham. He then reclaimed control of his see city and, having shriven Litster, led him to the gallows. This action effectively concluded the Peasants' Rebellion in Norfolk.

Although vigilantly suppressed, the Peasants' Rebellion was instrumental in raising issues that had to be addressed for the health of both the economy and the social stability of the emerging nation. The movement toward the ending of serfdom continued in spite of the suppression of the rebellion, and the agricultural society began to transform itself into a three-tiered hierarchy of freeholders, tenant farmers, and landless (or near-landless) laborers.

The agrarian economy was in the midst of an adjustment from primarily animal husbandry to arable farming, which was more profitable and less labor intensive. The unemployment thus caused led to a migration to the towns and cities, which, in Norwich's case, offered a wide variety of alternative employment.

Thus the Peasants' Rebellion was a symptom of the major changes that were taking place in the economy and social structure of England in the second half of the fourteenth century, changes with which we will become more familiar as we turn our attention to the city of Norwich as Julian would have known it.

2

Norwich in the
Second Half of the Fourteenth Century

The City

Norwich in the second half of the fourteenth century was the second city in the land after London, in terms of both its population (approximately thirteen thousand) and its wealth, the principal ingredient of which was a dominant position in the wool trade. Norwich was the nucleus of trade with the Netherlands and Europe and had already become renowned for its specialty of worsted cloth, which originated in the town of Worstead, outside Norwich. It would be wrong, however, to think of Norwich only in terms of the wool trade, just as there is little evidence that the large number of churches within the city can be attributed to the wealth of wool merchants alone.

As the map on page 26 indicates, Norwich was a heart-shaped walled city, approximately one mile and a quarter from north to south and one mile from east to west. The River Yare and its tributary, the Wensum, gave the city direct access to Great Yarmouth and the North Sea routes to the Continent. The city skyline in the fourteenth century would have been dominated by two structures: the cathedral and the castle.

The cathedral and the Benedictine priory attached to it were at the center of everything that happened in Norwich. Four hundred and seven feet long, with a spire soaring to a height of 315 feet, the cathedral building was begun in 1097 by Herbert de Losinga, the first Bishop of Norwich. It remains in substantially the same form today, including a bishop's throne standing high above and behind the altar, a survival from medieval times that is unique. Little of the main buildings of the priory survives, but the magnificent and extensive cloister gives the contemporary visitor a dramatic hint of the size of the priory until its destruction during the Dissolution of the Monasteries, at which time the stones of the priory were used to construct many of the beautiful homes that make up the current cathedral close. The friars became canons of the surviving cathedral and moved into what were presumably superior accommodations in the new close. In Julian's time the priory flourished and was indeed

Norwich Cathedral
Southeast View

(*The Cathedrals of England, Hürlimann*)

the cause of struggles with the laity, which will concern us as we examine the role of the church in Norwich.

Shortly after the Battle of Hastings in 1066, the Normans built a wooden fort on a mound above the city in Norwich. By about 1100 this was replaced by one of the largest and strongest stone keeps in England. By the thirteenth century, it was used primarily as a prison, a role it retained for five hundred years. As late as 1867, public hangings still took place at the castle gates.

Within its walls during the fourteenth century, the city contained fifty-four churches, a figure surpassed only by London and Lincoln, and four large friaries belonging to the Augustinian, Carmelite, Dominican, and Franciscan orders.

Some forty-six craft guilds and pious confraternities are recorded as having been in existence in this period, and Norman Tanner (pp. 205-207) lists ninety-one different crafts that were in operation between 1370 and 1532.

Articifers & operators
Bakers
Barbers
Barkers
Basket-makers
Bed-weavers
Bellfounders
Bowers
Braziers
Brewers
Broiderers
Butchers
Calenderers
Candlemakers
Cappers
Cardmakers
Carpenters
Carriers
Claymen
Cobblers
Collar-makers
Cooks
Coopers
Cordwaners
Coverlet-weavers
Curriers
Dornick-weavers
Drapers
Dyers
Fishers
Fishmongers
Fletchers
Fullers
Glaziers
Glovers
Gold-beaters
Goldsmiths
Gravers
Grocers
Haberdashers
Hardwaremen
Hatters
Hosiers
Innkeepers
Joiners
Keelmen

Lime-burners
Masons
Mercers
Millers
Minstrels
Parchmenters
Parish clerks
Patyn-makers
Peltiers
Pewterers
Physicians
Pinners
Plumbers
Point-makers
Pursers
Raffmen
Reders
Redesellers
Sawers
Scriveners
Sextons
Shearmen
Shoemakers
Sieve-makers
Skeppers
Skinners
Smiths
Spurriers
Stainers
Surgeons
Tailors
Tanners
Thatchers
Thickwoollen weavers
Tilers
Turners
Vintners
Waits
Watermen
Wax chandlers
Wheelwrights
Wiredrawers
Wool-chapmen
Woollen-weavers
Worsted-weavers

From this list we gain a detailed impression of a busy city, filled with large numbers of craftsmen plying their trades. Crafts associated with the wool trade do predominate, but one also notes such diverse skills as those used by saddlers and spur makers, brewers, goldsmiths, keelmen, minstrels, parchmenters, thatchers and sieve makers, not to dwell on the more esoteric cordwaners, raffmen, and skeppers! Much of the sense of bustling activity may be gained from visiting the open market, still in operation today in Norwich. Hundreds of stalls, huddled closely together with narrow, crowded passages between them, protected by tent-like canvas roofing, offer merchandise as varied as their medieval predecessors'. Fish and chips, clothing, and the latest in inexpensive digital watches are offered at what one is assured by the seller are prices that constitute the bargain of the century. The general level of noise, the aroma of cooking and farm produce, and the jostling of the determined shoppers cannot have changed significantly in the last six hundred years.

Norwich in the fourteenth century was a flourishing city. Its broad diversity of commerce guaranteed its survival regardless of the fluctuations in any particular market, although any major variation in the wool trade must have been felt and competition from the Continent must have been a continuing threat, similar to that of the Japanese import business which challenges local manufacture in our own time.

The mayor and aldermen notwithstanding, the major force in the city was in Julian's era the church, and it is to this omnipresent institution that we now turn our attention.

The Church

The church in Norwich in Julian's time reflects many characteristics that would later be regarded as typical of post-Reformation Anglicanism. With a strong sense of the continuing tradition it had inherited, the church nevertheless broke much new ground in its piety and practice during the fourteenth century, including a major growth in the anchorite movement, of which Julian can claim to be an early and prime example. The individual anchorite was enclosed permanently in his or her own cell, which was not necessarily connected to any particular religious order or institution. The anchorite was literally "anchored" by a vow of stability to one place, into which he or she had been sealed by the officiating bishop, and was from then on treated as dead to the world, having been the subject of a requiem mass.

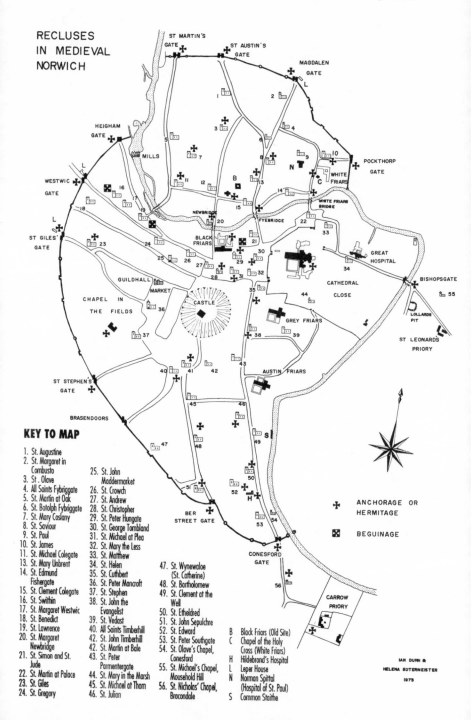

RECLUSES
IN MEDIEVAL
NORWICH

KEY TO MAP

1. St. Augustine
2. St. Margaret in Combusto
3. St . Olave
4. All Saints Fybriggate
5. St. Martin at Oak
6. St. Botolph Fybriggate
7. St. Mary Coslany
8. St. Saviour
9. St. Paul
10. St. James
11. St. Michael Colegate
12. St. Mary Unbrent
13. St. Edmund Fishergate
14. St. Clement Colegate
15. St. Swithin
16. St. Margaret Westwic
17. St. Benedict
18. St. Lawrence
19. St. Margaret Newbridge
20. St. Simon and St. Jude
21. St. Martin at Palace
22. St. Giles
23. St. Gregory

25. St. John Maddermarket
26. St. Crowch
27. St. Andrew
28. St. Christopher
29. St. Peter Hungate
30. St. George Tombland
31. St. Michael at Plea
32. St. Mary the Less
33. St. Matthew
34. St. Helen
35. St. Cuthbert
36. St. Peter Mancroft
37. St. Stephen
38. St. John the Evangelist
39. St. Vedast
40. All Saints Timberhill
41. St. John Timberhill
42. St. Martin at Bale
43. St. Peter Parmentergate
44. St. Mary in the Marsh
45. St. Michael at Thorn
46. St. Julian

47. St. Wynewaloe (St. Catherine)
48. St. Bartholomew
49. St. Clement at the Well
50. St. Etheldred
51. St. John Sepulchre
52. St. Edward
53. St. Peter Southgate
54. St. Olave's Chapel, Conesford
55. St. Michael's Chapel, Mousehold Hill
56. St. Nicholas' Chapel, Bracondale

B   Black Friars (Old Site)
C   Chapel of the Holy Cross (White Friars)
H   Hildebrond's Hospital
L   Leper House
N   Norman Spital (Hospital of St. Paul)
S   Common Staithe

✠   ANCHORAGE OR HERMITAGE

▦   BEGUINAGE

IAN DUNN &
HELENA SUTERNEISTER
1975

This movement owes its origins to a time at least as far back as Antony of Egypt (ca. A.D. 300) and continues to the present day, usually in much modified form, particularly in the Eastern Orthodox tradition.

Had you stopped the man or woman of Norwich on the street and asked this citizen to describe his or her faith, I suspect the answer would have been, "I'm a Christian, of course!" accompanied by a look of disbelief that anyone would ask a question whose answer was so obvious. The church was encountered at every major passage through life—at birth, marriage, and death. The church was also responsible for what we would now describe as all aspects of health, education, and welfare. Schools, hospitals, and the care and feeding of the poor, the elderly and all in need were the responsibility of the church. Its ability to perform these functions was enhanced by two considerations. First, an assured place in paradise was still regarded as the direct result of the charitable works undertaken in this life. Second, the church, through the person of the parish priest, who had the benefit of literacy, was responsible for the preparation of wills. A high percentage of these wills not unnaturally contained provision for the continued well-being of the testator's parish. We also need to remember that a church that pervaded so many of the functions of daily life was also totally integrated into all the functions of government, and those who find the continuing "established" nature of the Church of England quaint must be aware that the pluralism of England today was unknown in the fourteenth century, pluralism being the holding of more than one benefice or parish living. With the suppression of the Jews in 1290, Norwich became a "one-church city," notwithstanding a choice of over fifty parish churches. It must also be remembered that in England, then as now, parish boundaries, like diocesan boundaries, were geographical and parish registers contained the names of all citizens living within those boundaries, whether those listed ever darkened the doors of the parish church or not. Absenteeism seems not to have been a major problem in the fourteenth century, but this is hard to quantify because it is possible that incumbents allowed a status quo of low attendance to prevail without making any effort to correct such lapses in Christian commitment. The accuracy of parish records would presumably have borne a direct relationship to the efficiency with which the incumbent processed the collection of tithes, upon which, in most cases, he would be heavily reliant for his living.

The church in England was, in the fourteenth century, a branch of the worldwide Roman Catholic Church. Yet it had retained a proud degree of independence through most of its existence, an independence which, it will be remembered, encouraged Pope Gregory to send Augustine to Canterbury many centuries earlier. Rome was still the central power, but the growth of the monarchy and the concept of the nation-state was already causing a tension that was to reach its point of crisis under Henry VIII in the breach with Rome. The hierarchy was simple, at least on paper. The church in England was divided into two provinces, Canterbury and York, presided over by their respective archbishops. The primacy of Canterbury was already a hard-won reality in this period. Below the level of the province was the diocesan see under the control of the diocesan bishop, whose powers were extensive, and it was not for nothing that these powerful men were to be known as "princes of the church." They were assisted by suffragan or assisting bishops, again, identified by geographical location, sometimes foreign and purely honorary, but under the direct supervison of the diocesan bishops, who were jealous of their personal powers and prerogatives. The bishops further delegated considerable power to their archdeacons, who in turn were served by rural deans (selected from among the parish clergy), who made up the vast majority of the secular clergy (as distinguished from the "regular clergy"). Regular clergy lived under a monastic rule, and might have been either monks or friars, depending upon which order they embraced.

In spite of the rich and varied opportunities for worship and piety beyond the confines of the local parish church, especially available in a city such as Norwich, the parish church remained the core of the individual's expression of faith. It was also the individual's connection to the universal church, united throughout the civilized world of the age by its common liturgy and language—Latin—and owing allegiance to its principal bishop, the bishop of Rome, St. Peter's successor, the pope. The Great Schism, whereby the papacy was in 1378 divided into two contesting claimants at Rome and at Avignon, did much to weaken the authority of the papacy during the fourteenth century.

The immediate center of power was the diocese. In England at this time there were seventeen dioceses: Canterbury, Carlisle, Chichester, Durham, Ely, Exeter, Hereford, Lincoln, London, Norwich, Rochester, Salisbury, Winchester, Worcester, York, Bath and Wells, and Lichfield and Coventry, these last two having been combined previously. Wales contained four additional dioceses: Bangor, Llandaff, St. Asaph, and St. David's. These dioceses controlled some nine thousand parishes, which varied enormously in size from the large and extremely wealthy major city churches, to the smallest rural parish church that was little more than a family chapel in which members of a manorial estate worshiped as a small community. Church buildings of this period with a capacity for less than twenty-five worshipers are still plentiful today, leading to a twentieth-century pluralism in which it is not unknown for one clergyman to be responsible for at least six parish churches, and there are even instances of clergy caring for as many as ten places of worship.

The tradition of the church in the fourteenth century as to liturgy and worship would today be described as being on the "high" end of the scale of churchmanship, with evidence of elaborate ritual and vestments. The medieval piety of Norwich sought expression in a rich variety of ways: the veneration of saints; the belief in the effectiveness of masses and chantries for the deceased; the importance of pilgrimages, of which Chaucer's renowned account offers us a lively, if somewhat cynical view; the responsibility for crusades against the infidel and, indeed, the schismatic; the performance of mystery plays; frequent processions; membership in any number of pious confraternities; interest in a deep personal mysticism; and last, but by no means least in the light of this work's purpose, a remarkable growth in vocations to the eremetical and anchoritic life. The church provided a rich tapestry into which the individual's piety would be woven, a variety of expression that survived the Reformation and still rejoices in that most Anglican of concepts the *via media*—the "middle way"—which in my understanding, is already in abundant evidence in the theology of Julian and the breadth of the Christian experience in the Norwich of her day. The church was already on the road to the Reformation, but it never abandoned its appreciation of the health gained by keeping the forces of continuity and development in balance. Norman Tanner expresses it thus:

> The Reformation in Norwich is seen as a development from within the late medieval Church as much as a reaction against it. Otherwise it is difficult to explain why the religion of a city that appears to have been in a healthy state was jettisoned within two generations (Tanner, p.171).

The Parish

The parish was the center of life during the fourteenth century, but the extent to which this center was taken for granted, except in times of great need, is impossible to establish. A Martian visiting a village in England even today might well gain the impression that the parish church is the center of all that happens. Usually the largest and most dominant building in the area, the church continues to draw its geographical parishioners to itself for major family events—baptisms, weddings, funerals—and these are appropriately recorded for posterity. Should our Martian gain access to the attendance records, a different story might emerge. We do not have attendance records for the fourteenth century, but the absence of comment leads us to suppose that although there may well have been a measure of absenteeism, major obligations were probably met by a majority. The laity were obliged to hear mass on Sundays and feast days in their own church, and to receive penance and the eucharist at least once a year from their parish priest. They were also obliged to pay their tithes and offer oblations to their parishes. The fact that many of the parishes in Norwich had already been combined by this date indicates that attendance at the weekly masses may have become spasmodic. Julian's own church, St. Julian's, was already combined with St. Edward's and was to be further combined with St. Clement of Conesford at the end of the fifteenth century. That many of the feast days were accompanied by processions and activities by the guilds and pious confraternities might have encouraged attendance, although this would often involve presence at the cathedral rather than at a particular parish church. Many of the pious confraternities were attached to particular parishes, but their very number suggests that they tended to be small and not a major influence on attendance. The largest confraternities were attached to the two colleges, to the cathedral, and to the four friaries. Nevertheless, the parish churches remained the nuclei of regular worship and adherence to the sacraments.

Baptism, matrimony, extreme unction, penance, the eucharist, religious instruction, the hearing of the mass, the churching of women, and the visitation of the sick would have continued as part of the daily round in the parish context. The availability of a bishop and a large number of both secular and regular priests would have left the citizen with little excuse for delaying the rites of baptism and confirmation, although the fact that confirmation was not a prerequisite for the reception of communion makes it likely that confirmation was not as universal as it later became within our tradition. Marriages, as today in England, normally took place in the parish church. There were probably cases of common-law marriage, without benefit of the church's blessing, but I suspect that social pressure made these arrangements comparatively rare and confined to those for whom the fees involved for engaging the priest's services proved too burdensome. This does not, however, mean that marriage was universally held to be an inviolable and sacred trust in which the oath of fidelity was considered sacrosanct. The court records of the time indicate widespread infidelity and immorality in the city of Norwich, with the clergy in no way immune to prosecution. There must have been considerable reliance on the efficacy of confession and absolution in this area of activity.

The eucharist was seen as the central act of worship, and the tradition in the diocese of Norwich was what would be described as "high church." An inventory of vestments from St. Peter Mancroft in 1368 included the following, indicating a strong eucharistic liturgical tradition: ten sets of vestments for priest, deacon, and subdeacon; fourteen other sets of vestments; nine frontispieces for the altar; eight chalices; four banners; four thuribles; seven missals; six breviaries; and three psalters.

One does not have ten sets of eucharistic vestments and four thuribles unless one intends to make use of them on a regular basis. It is also likely that the level of high and low churchmanship varied from parish to parish, as it does in many cities today, so that in spite of the geographical obligation already referred to, one who sought a particular liturgical style could surely find it among the approximately fifty alternative places of worship.

Penance, which preceded the reception of the eucharist, was seen as an opportunity not only for absolution from sin, but also for instruction in the Christian virtues and way of life. Much instruction was by rote, necessitated by the general lack of literacy. The catechism is a good example of how this form of instruction was achieved: both the questions and the appropriate answers were memorized. Hearing mass did not necessarily involve receiving the eucharist, which demanded confession in advance, so that we may envision normative attendance as going to church to hear the mandatory portions of the mass, without receiving the eucharist and possibly avoiding the benefit of such preaching as may have been performed in the context of the mass. This preaching varied in quality according to the educational level of the preacher. There is evidence of a competitive element in preaching in Norwich between the secular clergy, the friars, and the regular clergy. Thomas Brinton, at one time a monk at the Cathedral Priory of Norwich, went on to become a nationally known preacher, eventually achieving the bishopric of Rochester. The prior of Gloucester College, Oxford, accused the friars, at about 1360, of preaching "against the norm of sound doctrine and the liberty of the church." The absence of major comment on preaching would, however, lead one to suppose that it was neither brilliant nor offensive. This was not an age that produced a large number of renowned preachers, a fact that may explain why, according to Norman Tanner's research, only three people are known to have left bequests to improve preaching between 1370 and 1532 (Tanner, p.11). It would be overoptimistic to suggest that the absence of such bequests signifies that the craft had already reached perfection in fourteenth century Norwich.

In the last of life's passages, the Christian citizen was entitled to burial from the church. There was a choice to be made between one's own parish church, the friaries, and the cathedral itself. Since the parish priest would have typically been responsible for the recording of the wishes of the deceased, during the preparation of a will, it is likely that any who made use of the priest's services for the preparation of his or her will would have been encouraged to seek burial within the parish. The fairly common practice of burial under the auspices of the friars leads to the suggestion that this alternative may have been attractive to those whose parish connections were tentative, further evidence of spasmodic attendance if not total absenteeism. Burial at the cathedral was restricted among the laity, as might be readily imagined, to those with considerable wealth. Many secular clergy chose not to be buried in their particular parishes. This might have been due to their close association with either the colleges where they had been trained or with the cathedral itself, which was, after all, the center of the diocese and the seat of their bishop, the pastor of the pastors.

As has been stated, the parish clergy were responsible for the preparation of their parishioners' wills. *The Book of Common Prayer* proclaims to this day the responsibility of Christians in making a will, fulfilling their obligations to their immediate family, and making provision for the church's well-being. In the fourteenth century, in some dioceses, it was mandatory to name one's parish in a will. This was not true of Norwich, but we would be foolish to suppose that a parish clergyman assisting a parishioner in the preparation of a will did not have at least his parish's, if not his own, interests at the forefront of his mind on such an occasion. Indeed, in Norwich the friars are known to have become involved in this function, in spite of the fact that in most rules this was expressly forbidden. Doubtless, the orders were able to overlook such indiscretions in the light of their clearly beneficial outcome to the institution.

Wills survive from 1370 in Norwich, where they were proved in the Norwich Consistory Court. From the period of Norman Tanner's study, 1370 to 1532, 1,804 wills survive. Tanner examined a sample of 615 of the 1,515 wills made by laity and all of the 289 made by the secular clergy (Tanner, pp. 220-225).

In many parts of the country, custom required that one-third of one's personal goods went to a surviving wife (testators were at this time presumed to be male), one-third went to any surviving children, and one-third (known as "Death's Part") was left to the discretion of the testator. Although this was common law in England at least up until the early thirteenth century, there is no clear reference to such practice in Norwich wills. Parish priests were instrumental in the construction and contents of wills. In addition to bequests for masses and prayers, preaching and scholarships, bequests are found for votive lights, religious houses, parish churches and clergy, hermits, anchorites and communities resembling beguinages, craft guilds and pious confraternities, hospitals, prisoners, and charitable works and civic projects, including but not limited to road maintenance and the upkeep of bridges. Eighty-five per cent of the clergy and ninety-five per cent of the laity whose wills were examined gave to at least one parish church and Tanner draws the following conclusion:

> In short, the wills of both the laity and the clergy give an impression of considerable enthusiasm for the parish churches of the city: to rebuild and adorn them, and to provide them with the liturgical items needed for celebrating services. This enthusiasm indicates their continuing vitality in the late Middle Ages, despite the arrival of houses of religious orders and colleges of secular priests and of new religious movements with a special appeal to the laity (Tanner, p.129).

Tanner concludes his review of testamentary bequests with a further instructive summary:

> The support given to the various branches of the Church reflects fairly accurately their importance in the religious life

of the city. Parish churches and houses of religious orders were especially well supported, and there were lesser flows of bequests to confraternities and to hermits and anchorites. The difference reflects the fact that the latter were important but never replaced the old institutions as the mainstay of the local Church, and that these older institutions appear to have retained considerable vitality and appeal (Tanner, p.140).

Tanner's statements go far to support my contention that the parish remained the focus of religious practice in Norwich during the time under consideration. It is also clear that Norwich tended toward conservatism in religious matters and greeted change with interest, but not at the cost of its loyalty to the church's historical tradition.

Within the parish structure, it is clear that the laity were in this period beginning to assume a role of increased involvement and a greater measure of control. Emma Mason, in *The Role of the English Parishioner, 1100-1500*, (pp. 25-29), argues that the laity were gaining control of parishes well before the Reformation, and the lay involvement in pious confraternities certainly supports this contention. Records of parish visitations by bishops also include regular instances of criticisms by laity, once they were invited, and they also demonstrate the responsibility the laity felt for the care, repair, maintenance, and rebuilding of the parish structures under their charge or control. In most instances the clergy were responsible for the chancel, and the laity for the remainder of the structure. In practice, it seems unlikely that either party would allow the other to neglect its portion of the required obligation, though there must have been instances when both parties, often for economic reasons, were guilty of neglect of the building.

The ability to maintain the plant of the parish buildings must have been heavily dependent on the successful collection of the tithes due. Indications are that most Christians fulfilled their obligations in this period, with negligence appearing to be more of a problem than outright refusal. Resistance to the tithe did increase in the fourteenth and fifteenth centuries, although records of episcopal visitations include only one reference to failure to pay tithes. Problems did arise, however, over the definition of parish and other boundaries, and the cathedral priory was often at the center of disputes, as we shall learn later. Because the priory was patron to more parishes than any other body, such disputes were, by definition, almost inevitable.

That Norwich was so amply supplied with clerical brethren of every type and description, many wielding enormous power within the church, leads me to suggest that Norwich was probably not in the vanguard of the church's movement toward giving the laity an increased role in the direction of its affairs, but rather followed the innovators along at a suitably conservative pace.

In summary, the parish churches in the fourteenth century were not only the center of Christian religious practice, but appear to have been flourishing and far from the exigencies of decline and decay that have sometimes been associated with this pre-Reformation period.

The Clergy

In addressing the state of the clergy in Julian's time, I will at this point be dealing with the secular clergy. The regular clergy, that is those under a rule, also called the "religious," and friars are the subject of discussion at a later stage in this study.

Norwich was at this time unusual in the large number of clergy of all types with which the citizens came into daily contact. Indeed, it must have been impossible to venture out into the narrow city streets without encountering significant numbers of the clergy going about their tasks, pastoral and otherwise. The prime responsibility of the secular clergy was to keep the laity reminded of the Christian way of life in a world that, like our own, must have contained a fair measure of distractions and temptations. The priest was seen as the mediator between God and humanity in the continual struggle for the redemption of the soul and the lightening of the much-feared burden of a prolonged passage through purgatory. Given his perceived ability to be instrumental in securing a more rapid passage through the supposed horrors of this state, by which lack of perfection in this life was corrected in preparation for the heavenly banquet, the priest held literally awesome spiritual power over his charges.

In the 1370s, England had something in excess of 25,000 secular clergy. This number suffered a temporary decline as a result of the previously discussed Black Death, but by the beginning of the fifteenth century the numbers were back to those obtaining before the plague. While we do not have accurate figures for Norwich in the same period, it is likely that the numbers remained reasonably stable, given the static nature of the jobs available, so that we might project that in the 1370s there would be some 125 secular priests in the city. Norwich was particularly badly affected by the plague and, following its return in 1369, clergy strength reached its nadir, at which point more than half the clergy had perished. Following the first outbreak in 1349, eleven benefices had received new incumbents within the year 1349-50, among which three benefices had been renewed twice within the year.

From where were the clergy recruited? The ranks of the secular clergy were chiefly what might be described as gentry or middleclass yeomen. Ordinands had to be freeborn and legitimate, although these two requirements could be eliminated through manumission and papal dispensation, respectively—time-consuming and probably costly processes. Wealthy townsmen would certainly have been able to qualify as clergy. Most of the clergy of this period appear to have been natives of Norwich, in distinction to the monks, who came from all over the country, and the friars, many of whom came even from abroad; this may be an explanation for the animosity that sometimes arose against the regular clergy and the Cathedral Priory itself. It was not at this time considered normative for the younger sons of aristocratic families to join the church, although a clerical career does not seem to have been considered in any way inappropriate.

The first step toward a clerical career was to receive the first tonsure, which signified clerical status and not much else. It may have depended on a simple degree of literacy, but seems to have been more of a rite of passage that did not necessarily lead to advancement to Holy Orders. Could it have been a form of fallback position for young men, an informal variety of employment insurance? We must remember that education was in the hands of the church, and therefore encouragement toward taking the first tonsure may have been part of the pressure a young man would undergo as he neared the end of his schooling.

A career in the church, given the appropriate credentials, was probably relatively easy to pursue. The growth in linked parishes during this period must in part have been caused by a scarcity of qualified parish clergy, as well as by the decimation caused by the Black Death. There were other opportunities that attracted secular clergy away from parochial employment. Among these were chantries, positions within collegiate churches, and chaplaincies of guilds and pious confraternities. However, some of these tasks were being assumed by parochial clergy as sources of additional income, notwithstanding the theoretical restrictions concerning pluralism, of which more will be said later. Progress up and through the ranks was usually slow. One either received a benefice shortly after ordination or tended to join the vast number of unbeneficed clergy, whose chances of subsequent elevation to the rank of beneficed clergy were not high. It would often take up to ten years to achieve this state. Promotion was rarely based on merit, but was affected by various influences, few of which had anything to do with the quality or depth of the cleric's vocation. In an occupation that had developed its own practices, the clergy must have been under heavy pressure to conform to the system, far though it might have traveled from any Christian ideal. There was a ready market in benefices for those who could afford the price, and those who engaged in the business of brokering these opportunities were known as "chop-churches." Pluralism was a reality, as it has become in our own day, but did not necessarily lead to abuse. A further pressure was the need to secure a living that would provide a sufficient pension to care for the clergyman following retirement. Failure to achieve this would lead to eventual resort to the hospitals and almshouses that were shared with the sick and the indigent. Secular clergy in the wealthier parishes of Norwich did not need to fear this eventuality, but for the vast majority of unbeneficed clergy, life was lived out at close to subsistence level.

R.N. Swanson, in his *Church and Society in Late Medieval England*, gives a good summary of the state of clergy at the time:

> The abilities and quality of the clergy also need to be assessed, matters which vexed contemporary laity and ecclesiastical authorities as much as later historians. Unfortunately, it is not absolutely clear just what was required of would be clerics. The pre-ordination examinations which are known to have occurred yield few indications of what was demanded, or how effectively the candidates were assessed. The monitions issued to ordinands specify only technical qualifications: they should be free-born, legitimate, unmarried, not bigamists (not having married twice, or have married a widow), not be homicides, not be seeking advancement by simony or fraud, and have sufficient title (means of support) or appropriate letters dimissory if being ordained outside their native diocese. There is no mention of ability or vocation (Swanson, p.58).

From this quotation, it can be seen that there is a degree of uncertainty regarding the level of competence required for the would-be clergy to qualify. I suspect that then, as now, the standards varied significantly from diocese to diocese, depending to some extent on need and the ever-present laws of supply and demand. In any event, some degree of literacy was essential, along with a modicum of competence in Latin, critical in a church which required that services be conducted in Latin, not to mention one whose administration was also conducted in that language. Such ability in Latin was tested; there are known instances of bishops refusing to ordain candidates before they had completed further studies in Latin. Many of the clergy were clearly well educated and well read. Evidence of clergy's possession of sophisticated libraries occurs in many of their wills. Nationally, it is estimated that between one-third and one-half of the clergy in the fourteenth century attended a university. The figures for Norwich in this period are not as optimistic. Between 1370 and 1449, only 12 of 158 rectors or vicars are known to have been university graduates, but this does not take into account those who studied at the universities without taking a degree or those whose university education took place without formal records surviving. During the fifteenth century, with the growth in the universities, this figure for Norwich improves measurably.

Training for Norwich clergy might well have begun at the secondary-school level, at one of three schools: the Song School, the Almery School (both of which were attached to the Cathedral Priory), or the Grammar School. From there it would be possible to study at one of the four secular "colleges" in Norwich: the College of St. Mary in the Fields, the Carnary College, the College of the Chantry Priests in the bishop's palace, or the college attached to St. Giles Hospital. These colleges were organizations of secular priests, with whom it would be possible to "read for orders," an alternative that was also accomplished through becoming attached, as it were, as an apprentice to an active parish clergyman. For some there followed a period at Oxford or Cambridge University, both of which had the patronage of parishes in Norwich, but must be remembered as being very limited in size as compared with their present-day counterparts. In 1360 two monks from the cathedral priory were known to be studying at Gloucester College, the Benedictine house at Oxford. These two monks, Adam Easton and Thomas Brinton, were to proceed far in their clerical careers, the former attaining the rank of cardinal and the latter becoming bishop of Rochester. Cardinal Easton was instrumental in enhancing the already magnificent library at the cathedral priory, when he bequeathed 228 books to the priory in 1407. By the time of the Dissolution, this library contained at least 1,350 volumes.

All this education was naturally available formally only to male students. However, the close proximity of both the priory library and the libraries of the friaries, particularly the Augustinian house, prompts one to wonder whether Julian did not gain access to this theological wealth, if only through an intermediary. Young girls would either have been educated by the nuns at Carrow Nunnery, as either day students or boarders, or have received tutoring from a private chaplain, had their parents sufficient means to afford this luxury.

Probably long before completion of the appropriate educational preparation, the priest-in-training would be concerned with the critical matter of patronage, without which a life of unbeneficed poverty was a serious prospect. Positions could be bought through payment of money, in spite of the official restrictions imposed on this system of simony. Patronage was the universal method of appointment to benefices. Patrons could be individuals, families, or institutions. Although between 1350 and 1540 papal patronage declined and became almost totally extinguished, in the mid-fourteenth century it still had a part to play. Bishops controlled some livings, although this situation was not prevalent in Norwich. By far the most important and prestigious patron was the Crown, although in Norwich the king held the patronage of only one parish. In Norwich, easily the most powerful patron was the Cathedral Priory, which held twenty-one benefices. A considerable distance behind the priory, the College of St. Mary in the Fields came next, with only four. Carrow Nunnery held three benefices and the rest were distributed between Oxford and Cambridge colleges, parishes from beyond Norwich, and a variety of institutions, families, and individuals. The Statute of Provisors in 1351 seriously limited papal ability to interfere in matters of appointment. The crown was happy to assume this role and retains it to this day, especially with respect to the appointment of bishops, a prerogative which, in the fourteenth century, found royal patronage at its most significant.

Bishops in this period were either noblemen or extremely well-connected gentry. They not only served as "princes of the church," but were also responsible for the functions of civil servants, diplomats, members of the royal household, and lawyers, both in the ecclesiastical and the crown courts. Bishops were appointed by cathedral chapters, operating under instructions from the Crown. The majority of bishops were university graduates, either in theology or law. The bishops of Norwich were by definition wealthy, and the occupant of the bishop's throne in

Norwich for much of the period with which we are concerned was the colorful Henry Despenser, who occupied the see from 1370 until 1406. Not only was he ruthless in his suppression of the Peasants' Rebellion and his treatment of any potential heretics, but he gained considerable notoriety by leading a military "crusade" against the schismatic Flemish in 1383. He had seen previous military service, but this did not prevent the crusade from becoming a disastrous and embarrassing failure, for which Despenser was rewarded with an attempted but unsuccessful impeachment. Despenser was followed by the less warlike Alexander Tottington, from 1406 until 1413, John Wakeryng from 1415 until 1425, and William Alnwick from 1426 until 1436—which takes us past the very latest possible date for Julian's death. These successors to Despenser were much involved in the maintenance of sound doctrine against claims of the followers of Wyclif and the Lollards, a movement we will cover later in this work.

As can be gathered from this broad survey of the state of the clergy in fourteenth-century Norwich, there were considerable abuses within the clergy at this time. However, I believe that there has been a tendency to exaggerate these abuses in order to explain the changes sought by the Reformation and to justify the mood of anticlericalism that prevailed nationally prior to the Reformation. There is scant if any indication of such anticlericalism in Norwich in this period. Indeed, it appears that in this city inundated with clergy, the clerical status quo seemed acceptable and at least tacitly endorsed by the lay population, many of whom doubtless gained from the commerce the ecclesiastical presence engendered.

Yet, abuses there were, and they followed the familiar patterns. Simony, or the purchase of offices for cash, was a fact of life. Nepotism reached extraordinary heights in this period, as in the example of the Booth family of Barton who, in the fifteenth century, produced two archbishops, two bishops, three archdeacons and one Dean of York.

Pluralism, the possession of multiple livings, frequently occurred, but as in today's practice, did not necessarily constitute abuse. Pluralism was often required to keep smaller parishes provided with clergy, if only on a part-time basis. Absenteeism by clergy, notably caused by nonresidence, did provoke some abuse, but here again the holders of benefices frequently secured the services of chaplains and unbeneficed clergy to perform the priestly functions on their behalf, thus creating jobs for lesser clergy. The ecclesiastical court records testify to a fair amount of immorality among both clergy and laity; the clergy were in no way immune to the temptations of the world, the flesh, and the devil. Loss of celibacy, clerical paternity, fornication, adultery, and the sexual abuse of minors all occurred with regularity. Norman Tanner provides two instances from accounts of episcopal visitations in Norwich that give substance to this less than laudable situation:

> Agnes Saunders fosters sexual immorality among priests, women, members of religious orders, canons, and all sorts (Tanner, p. 53).

> Brother John Caster is known to be unchaste with Isabel Chapman, junior (Tanner, p. 53).

Doubtless, local gossip eventually brought these situations to the attention of the visiting bishop. As today, stories of clerical misbehavior hold a peculiar attraction, but one should not allow the activities of a minority to besmirch an entire profession. In general, the paucity of complaints indicates that the clergy of Norwich were not especially prone to widespread abuse of their office, but functioned well and effectively.

In summation, from the bishops to the lowliest, unbeneficed clerical proletariat, struggling on the borders of literacy and subsistence, the church in this period was hierarchical and powerful. Movement between the ranks was far less common than it is today, an era in which an authentic Cockney has assumed the archbishopric of Canterbury. Within that hierarchy, however, was a basically competent clergy who provided the overwhelming majority of the social and pastoral needs of the medieval population, and did so reasonably honestly and effectively.

The Religious

As already suggested, Norwich in the time of Julian was teeming with members of the various religious orders. It has been calculated that some nine thousand religious existed nationally during this period. The number was at least halved by the Black Death, which affected the religious just as severely as the secular clergy, but the number of religious had recovered to its preplague level by 1420. Thus, the Black Death is not to be seen as the final blow to any enthusiasm for the religious life. That the numbers recovered at all is proof of the continuing popularity of this form of vocation. As for the actual numbers of religious in Norwich, we can be reasonably accurate in the case of the Cathedral Priory, with 60 monks in 1309 and a stable number of 50 between 1389 and 1460; Carrow Nunnery held no less than 9 and no more than 17 nuns at any one time during this period. For the rest of the institutions, records are less available, but we would not be far wrong to assume an aggregate population of approximately 150 in the second half of the fourteenth century, allowing for a significant drop during the ravages of the Black Death.

If one uses a broad interpretation of the word "religious," embracing anyone under some form of vow with a religious intent, Norwich can claim some twenty-six such institutions.

We gain a picture of a highly active and numerous religious community, involved in many areas of city life and responsible for much of the pastoral care of the population. Some tensions inevitably arose. The secular clergy objected to the friars' free-wheeling preaching style and content, presumably in part because the competition was proving popular with the populace. But the major conflicts, as already mentioned, sprang from the enormous power of the Cathedral Priory.

Conflict between the priory and the citizens was nothing new in the fourteenth century, but may have been exacerbated by the growing power of the mayor, the guilds, and the city govern-ment, which gained its royal charter in 1380. Ill feeling must have continued after the major outburst of 1272, when the citi-zenry mounted a full-scale assault on the Cathedral Priory, burn-ing several buildings and causing the death of thirteen persons. Retribution was brutal and ruthless. Thirty citizens were hanged for their part in the assault. Resentment of the wealth and power of the priory lay at the roots of the conflict. The priory appointed nearly half of the parish priests and was by far the most extensive owner of land both in the city and in the suburbs. Through its parish connections, the priory must have exerted power well beyond its technical boundaries, and it was these boundaries that formed the basis of much of the wrangling during the time which concerns us. Both through its wielding of temporal juris-dictions and its claim to exemptions from various levies, the pri-ory appeared to be doing too much of the taking and too little of the giving.

Rectors and parish chaplains found themselves at odds with the priory over the major procession that took place on the First Sunday after Trinity Sunday, a row that was eventually settled by Bishop Despenser in 1390. One suspects that the procession had become something of a shambles and that the clergy had begun to refuse to participate.

The priory, earlier described as in control of the cathedral, even ran afoul of the bishop over its respective rights of government and the "reverencialia" due to the bishop. This friction reached its height under the aggresive Bishop Despenser, who would not have enjoyed the competitive power of the reigning abbot.

There were doubtless many other issues that arose in the day-to-day life of this finely intermeshed society, but it is notable that the Cathedral Priory maintained a peaceful relationship with the friaries and the College of St. Mary in the Fields, institutions which one might have expected to provide further dispute. In that these foundations acquired little property during this period, there were perhaps few grounds for conflict. In 1368 the Augustinians incorporated the parish of St. Michael of Conesford into their site, but this was apparently a mutually agreeable and friendly action.

Minor incidents concerning jurisdiction continued throughout the period. An amusing situation arose in the case of a woman arrested by the city bailiffs in St. Paul's Parish in 1373, only to find herself being "stolen" back by the monks, who claimed jurisdiction over her.

By the beginning of the fifteenth century, the relationships between the priory and the other institutions, both lay and religious, appear to have gradually improved, as evidenced in the increased number of bequests made to the Cathedral Priory and the continuation of requests by prominent laity for burial within the cathedral precincts.

Throughout the nation at this time, there is some evidence of a decline in the standards of most of the religious foundations, with the notable exception of the Carthusians, who retained a reputation for a deep and authentic spirituality during this age. Interestingly, however, they had no Charterhouse in Norwich and the Carthusian influence on the city was thus minimal. Undoubtedly, the religious became increasingly involved in the secular, commercial, and economic affairs of the city. Absence from the mother houses and failure to maintain discipline among peers must have led to further weakening of the original standards of the rules, but none of these circumstances appear to have hastened a decline in the presence and efficacy of these major influences in the life of fourteenth-century Norwich. Chaucer's view of the religious may have had some good examples in this center of medieval spirituality, but the strong survival of most of the religious in Norwich until the Dissolution presupposes that their presence continued to be more than welcome in Julian's day.

3

The Church and the World in Julian's Time

The Church and Rome

Although we need to be continually reminded that the Church of England in the fourteenth century was the Church of Rome and that this connection forms the single most significant distinction between the Church of England then and now, we need also to remember that the church in England had through geographical and political means already achieved a considerable degree of independence from Rome. There was, however, a body of regular business that could be conducted only with Rome's assistance, and this business included, but was not limited to, dispensations for marriages, the appointment of confessors, dispensations for clerics (as in the matter of pronouncing legitimacy for those born out of wedlock), grants of indulgences, appeals of a variety of kinds, and at least a measure of influence in ecclesiastical appointments. Thus, although some independence had been achieved in most areas of the church's daily activity, there remained the constant tension of Rome's central control.

The Church and the State

R.N. Swanson, in his *Church and Society in Medieval England*, sets the stage for this discussion:

> Given its wealth, its international connections, and its virtual monopoly of learning until the fifteenth century, it was only natural that the church and its personnel should be firmly integrated into the political structure (Swanson, p. 103).

A somewhat extreme example of the intermingling of church

and state could be seen in Bishop Henry Despenser of Norwich's "Crusade" in the Netherlands in 1383. That a bishop should be leading military forces on behalf of the Crown, albeit identified with God's holy purpose, was not the reason for its being criticized. Despenser's problem was that he lost the battle in which he engaged.

While the connections between church and state were at this time multifaceted, change was in progress as a lay, secular view of state began to develop. The role of the church in state matters was no longer presumed. Royal power was beginning to be seen as derived directly from God, without full reliance upon the mediation of the institutional church. This demonstrates a belief in the theory of the divine right of kings, a theory that was to gain strength in direct proportion to the increasing power of the concept of monarchy.

The church was also deeply entangled in the collection of taxes, both secular and ecclesiastical, and in the dispensing of justice. In addition, the church was reponsible for the running of several mints, a function that suggests a careful reading of Christ's admonition to "render unto Caesar. . . ." Major conflicts arose over legal jurisdictions, and we will examine them in greater detail when we take a look at the church and the law in a later section.

It is clear that by this time the church and its clergy had become thoroughly embroiled in many of the intricacies of local government, at the expense of much of its higher calling, as Swanson describes the situation:

> That the church was so involved in local administration in the later Middle Ages, and that it enjoyed widespread franchised jurisdiction was important, but had little to do with its properly ecclesiastical functions (Swanson, p. 139).

The Church, Society, and Economics

There is no question that whether the motivation was occasioned by fear of prolonged sessions in purgatory or by a higher theological ideal, the wealthy felt a mandate toward practical charitable works on behalf of those in need, administered in most cases by the church. Those who had much were mindful of the moral imperative reflected in Christ's statement of Matthew 25:35-36: "I was hungry and you gave me food, I was thirsty and you gave me something to drink, I was a stranger and you welcomed me, I was naked and you gave me clothing, I was sick and you took care of me, I was in prison and you visited me."

Moving even beyond these expectations, we find the church assuming responsibility for all aspects of the people's welfare, supplying services we have long since expected from the secular authorities: education, feeding, housing, the care of the sick and the elderly, the ministration to prisoners and the protection and maintenance of the poor, not to mention the church's pastoral offices in time of family "passages," as in baptism, marriage, and burial. The evidence of wills and bequests suggests particular concern for neighbors, for defending widows and orphans (of whom there must have been a large number in the era of the Black Death), comforting the bereaved, helping the sick, and visiting the imprisoned. The Seven Corporal Acts of Mercy were seen as a guiding force throughout life. Even as death approached, they were not forgotten, charitable bequests being centered in four principal areas: chantries (prayers for the repose of the deceased and others), education, public works (including the care of those in need), and the maintenance and building of churches. Richard Caistor, a saintly Norfolk priest, made his interpretation of one's duty to the needy clear in his will, in which he stated, "The goods of the Church, according to Canon Law, belong to the poor" (Tanner, p. 136).

The church's influence on the economics of the period cannot be overstated. The church controlled between one-fifth and one-quarter of all the agricultural land in England in the Middle Ages. Religious houses often owned or leased land, and guilds and confraternities, heavily connected to the church, also owned much property. The church received major rental income in the towns, a fact that lay behind much of the tension between the Cathedral Priory and the people of Norwich.

The regular ecclesiastical functions of the church generated considerable income. Fees from baptisms, weddings, and funerals; indulgences; offerings at shrines; and guild membership fees all contributed to the church's coffers. Yet by far the greatest source of income for most segments of the church was the tithe, a form of ecclesiastical VAT (value added tax), which was levied on almost anything one might name: hay, wool, lambs, calves, piglets, geese, fruit, eggs, wood, honey, any agricultural product, and so on.

The church was actively involved in many aspects of the marketplace, not least of all as one of the major employers in the land. Through its elaborate organization and broad range of activities, the church was also instrumental in the circulation and redistribution of wealth, a healthy influence on the economy. Even the travel involved in pilgrimages and in conducting the affairs of the church would have boosted the economy in an early form of tourism.

Thus it can be seen that the church, society, and the economy of the Middle Ages are inseparable and interdependent, a far cry from the separation of church and state with which we are familiar in our day. The meeting point for many of the conflicts that arose from this mode of operation was often in matters of law, to which we now turn our attention.

The Church and the Law

The manner in which the two institutions, the monarchy and the church, developed was to a large extent responsible for the evolution of two distinct legal systems, which inevitably became competitive. Wherever a matter became the concern of both the Crown and the church, conflicts arose. There were many areas in which it was not easy to determine which institution should be awarded jurisdiction. Yes, the Crown claimed authority in matters of crime and property, but we have already established that the church was the greatest landowner after the king, and in matters of criminal activity, where morality was concerned, surely the church would have a valid claim. Thus the administration of justice was theoretically divided between the temporal and spiritual spheres. It is perhaps easiest to grasp how this distinction was made by describing the spiritual, which included all matters of ecclesiastical discipline for both lay persons and clergy: the implementation of church rights, including tithes and other fiscal obligations; the oversight of morality; marriage disputes and marital cases, sexual misbehavior, slander, wills, and all manner of business pertaining to oaths. One of the early problems arose over jurisdiction in property matters relating to benefices. Clearly the issues concerned property, which belonged to the Crown courts, but equally obviously, benefices were primarily an ecclesiastical concern and belonged in the church courts. Tithes, previously described as a form of ecclesiastical VAT, were described by the church as a fundamentally spiritual issue. The state claimed that tithes had purely to do with chattels. In the late fourteenth century a compromise was reached which evaded the question of definition, in which income from tithes became a secular issue only when they represented more than a quarter of the benefice's income. Needless to say, the interpretation of this compromise left the door open for fairly elastic interpretations of what represented a quarter and how income from a benefice was to be defined. The church courts maintained significant authority over matters pertaining to petty debt and wills. Invalid marriages and bastardy also continued to concern the church courts. To make the situation more complex, the church courts quite often had to appeal to the secular courts to implement the decisions they had reached. The intermingling of church and state, already observed in other areas, was in the area of law profound, and the conflict was not to be fully resolved until the Reformation.

Swanson summarizes and leads us toward a discussion of two principal areas in which the conflict came to the surface, benefit of clergy and sanctuary:

> The temporal was accepted as the crown's concern, the spiritual as the responsibility of the church. Where disputes occurred—rarely instigated by the kings themselves—was at the shared frontiers, as in the cases of sanctuary and benefit of clergy (Swanson, p. 182).

Benefit of clergy was a system by which those who could establish their clerical status could demand that, upon conviction in the secular courts, their cases could be transferred to the Church courts for disposition. As the Statute of 1352, *Pro Clero*, reads:

> All manner of clerks, seculars as well as regulars, who shall henceforth be convicted before secular justices for whatever felonies or treasons, concerning persons other than the king himself or his royal majesty, shall henceforth have and freely enjoy the privilege of holy church, and shall without hindrance or delay be handed over to the ordinaries who shall demand them (25 Edward III, s.6, c.3: Statutes, i, p. 325) (Swanson, p. 149).

The next issue to arise was the ability of the convicted to "prove his clergy," that is, to establish the validity of his claim to clerical status. This was achieved through a test of reading ability, on the presumption that literacy indicated clerical status, an indication of the universal grasp of the church in the realm of education.

The whole corpus of canon law developed from a complicated amalgamation of different sources. These need not concern us, other than to note that by the fourteenth century the canon law had become separated into two principal areas: "office" matters, which were those matters that were initiated by the church's own actions, and "instance" business, which had to do with what we would call "civil" cases, being tried before the church courts.

In their jurisdiction over spiritual matters, the calendars of the church courts seem to have been heavily weighed down by sexual offenses, which accounted for a very high percentage of all cases heard. The business of the church courts can be divided into three main areas of concern: breach of faith, defamation, and sexual or matrimonial matters. Heresy did not become a major issue in the church courts until the growth of Wyclifism and the Lollard movement, the suppression of which became a preoccupation of the courts in the early part of the fifteenth century. Continuing to exercise major influence in all matters pertaining to wills, bequests, and probate, the church courts were busy in this area, most particularly as related to moveables, as opposed to real property, which the secular courts regarded as their bailiwick.

There is no question of the broad extent of the grasp of the church courts, touching as they did on a wide range of activities having to do with the day-to-day existence of the average citizen. What is less clear is the extent to which the church courts were effective. Corruption was an ever-present problem, and the penalties the ecclesiastical courts might impose were inconsistent and in some cases temporary in their efficacy. Public flogging and demotion in public processions might have caused passing embarrassment, but would hardly have dissuaded a hardened offender. Offerings and fines may have been more effective, providing the offender had the means to pay them. Those with money could pay their way out of the public penalties described above. Pilgrimages were occasionally demanded as punishment, a difficult operation to oversee. Imprisonment was a real possibility for major offenses, and heresy could lead to execution. The church courts, however, would have to turn to the secular courts for the imposition of capital sentences. Excommunication and the Great Curse were penalties available to the church courts, the latter being a list of offenses, repeated four times annually in parish churches. Such offenses carried with them automatic excommunication upon discovery. Since the church lacked any real powers of physical coercion, my suspicion is that these penalties may have proved a deterrent principally to those least likely to commit the offenses, but that they would not have caused much pause in the actions of those determined to sin.

Swanson again summarizes well the coexistence between the secular and ecclesiastical systems:

> In the end, the problem of the relationship between the lay and the ecclesiastical courts resolved itself. The litigants were still there, but the remedies available to them had changed. The suitors voted with their feet, and in the search for "justice" took their business from the church's courts to the King's. The changes of the sixteenth century, even of the Reformation, did not extinguish ecclesiastical jurisdiction: the church courts, despite the turmoil of the Reformation years, were to recover and remain a force for some time, serving social purposes which they continued to fulfil (Swanson, p.190).

We thus can imagine a dual system in which the two parts managed to coexist peacefully most of the time. The conflicts, when they arose, had mainly to do with jurisdictional claims and were the exception rather than the rule. The system seems to have been one of mutual dependence and support, providing a fair degree of justice, but weighted inevitably toward the educated and those with sufficient wealth to affect the outcome to their own advantage—an accusation that can still be made of present-day systems of justice.

The Church and Spirituality in the World

There will be much more to be said about the spirituality of the Middle Ages as Julian's theology concerns us more specifically in the later parts of this book. At this point, it seems appropriate to give a broad view of the ways in which spirituality affected the daily existence of the citizens of Norwich in Julian's age. The whole of the fourteenth century was one in which mysticism flourished. Preoccupied with the extraordinary onslaughts of the Black Death and the uncertainty of life in a time of near-perpetual war, and threatened with dire consequences upon failure to adhere to the church's teaching, the common people were in awe of the prospect of death, and the consideration of death and its aftermath assumed cultic proportions. Even with fear predominating, there was, however, an ingredient of hope for those who had survived. The mere fact of survival was the subject of thanksgiving to God and might often lead to consideration of the purposes for which God had placed one in the world. Certainly, Julian contemplated this question as she sought to understand the full meaning of her visions. There was clearly a general theological stance in which faith and works were in tension as the means to salvation. It is apparent that lay involvement in spiritual matters increased during this period. The growth in pious confraternities and the religious activities of the guilds, all lay led, point to a general atmosphere of spiritual involvement. Church buildings were subject to multiple uses in a way that was perhaps not to reappear until the present century. The church's overwhelming presence in all aspects of an individual's life did not lead to a reaction of spiritual surfeit, but rather appears to have engendered tremendous hunger for spiritual sustenance and guidance. The popularity of Walter Hilton, Richard Rolle, and the anonymous author of *The Cloud of Unknowing* testifies to this demand, a demand which needed to be met in the vernacular English, in a country where theology had traditionally been communicated in Latin. Bequests of the period indicate that it was the laity who collected and read these English mystic writers in far greater numbers than did the clergy. The very appeal of the religious life in its rich variety of form adds to the picture of spiritual enthusiasm. By 1420, there were in England eight foundations established by the Carthusians, an order that emphasized spiritual discipline. Moreover, there were by this date at least 2,300 regular nuns in England, although, as noted earlier, few of them were to be found in Norwich.

At this time too, there were several differing opportunities for participation in the spiritual life for the lay person, outside the bounds of the regular religious orders. Formal religious instruction was sparse, confirmation being unnecessary for reception of communion. Such instruction as took place did so in the context of confession and absolution, through sermons, drama (especially in the form of mystery plays), spiritual literature (as discussed), pictures, songs, and various rituals, including the popular religious processions. These processions must have been a regular feature of city life. The various guilds and confraternities were responsible for the traveling mystery plays that were part of the processions. Norman Tanner lists twelve subjects that were the responsibility of various craft guilds, which give a good sense of the mobile enactments involved:

Creacion of the World, Helle Carte, Paradyse, Abell and Cayme, Noyse Shipp, Abraham and Isaak, Moises and Aron with the Children of Israell and Pharo with his Knyghtes, Conflicte of David and Golias, The Birth of Crist with Sheperdes and iii Kynges of Colen, The Baptysme of Criste, The Resureccion, and The Holy Gost (Tanner, p. 71).

The records of Norwich describe the mystery plays encountered on Whitmonday:

> . . . many disguisings and pageants of the lives and martyrdoms of many holy saints . . . and feigned figures and pictures of other persons and beasts . . . making a great circuit of the said city . . . (Hudson & Tingey, Vol.II, pp.311-313).

Paradise was amusingly described as "a pageant . . . on a four-wheel cart," something less than that which I hope to achieve as my final destination! (Davis, p.xxxv).

The elaborate nature of these processions is perhaps best illustrated by the cast of characters involved in the depiction of St. George slaying the dragon, provided by the Confraternity of St. George, which was the confraternity associated with the city government of Norwich. The pageant included a man on horseback, a model dragon—complete with fiery effects provided by gunpowder—and, in a sixteenth century development, a fair maiden on horseback. St. George and his immediate retinue were accompanied by the mayor and aldermen of the city, all mounted on horseback and in livery, and twenty-four priests, of whom twelve wore red copes and twelve wore white copes. The cathedral bells were rung throughout the procession, which was annexed to a service in the cathedral and subsequent feasting.

Given the large number of guilds and confraternities in the city of Norwich, one begins to gain an impression of the omnipresence of popular spirituality, which consistently inserted itself into the life of the city through displays of public enthusiasm. Today we might find such vulgar display of our faith embarrassing and inappropriate, but we are viewing the scene from a perspective in which faith has become a more private matter and in which religion is not considered part of the official establishment. Once again we are reminded that the church permeated society in the fourteenth century, and such opposition as there was failed to make any major inroads on the status quo. As we turn our attention to this opposition, it is interesting to note that the Lollards would not have approved of the practices just described, and to note further that their objections were not sustained, having little if any effect on the religious activities prevalent in Norwich.

The Church and Opposition

In the 1390s, a group of Cambridge doctors of divinity defined heresy as follows:

> Heresy is false dogma, contrary to the catholic faith and the determination of the church, which is pertinaciously defended. . . . A heretic is so named who discovers a new opinion or doctrine contrary to the faith or determination of the universal church, or to a proper understanding of the holy scriptures, or who follows such discoveries of others and pertinaciously defends them (Parry, p.393).

Heresy has ever been the crime associated with those who disagree with the establishment or the majority, though with the advantage of hindsight that history affords, one century's heretic becomes the next century's saint.

Opposition to the church in the fourteenth century to some degree sprang from the feeling among some that the gap between what the church preached and the way it acted was widening to the point at which it could no longer claim to be the true church, an accusation that is regularly made by dissidents and revolutionaries. As we will see, in the period in question, this accusation was not entirely without merit. It is my contention that the seeds of the Reformation are to be found well established in the fourteenth century and that those who were condemned as heretics in the last part of that century and the beginning of the fifteenth should be recognized as early protagonists in the struggle to achieve a reformed church, one that would be truer to its earlier nature than the established church of the time. I also believe that Julian can be counted among those who challenged the church establishment of her day to reform by returning to the principles of the earliest church. That she was not prosecuted as a heretic is a measure of the esteem in which she was held, for much of her theology runs counter to what was held to be orthodoxy at the time.

John Wyclif (ordained ca. 1356 and died 1384) was the leading proponent of doctrinal reform in this century in England, but it should be stressed that he favored reform from within the church and never intended any break from the church. It must also be understood that Wyclif would have been appalled by many of the excesses engaged in by the Lollards, with whom his name has been irretrievably linked. Indeed, Wyclif remained a beneficed, officiating priest until the time of his death, in spite of the fact that some of his arguments had been condemned by the Blackfriars Council in 1382.

Where, then, did Wyclif err? He denied transubstantiation and espoused a view of the eucharist based on the theory of remanence, in which it was held that the bread and the wine did not change materially at the time of their consecration, even if they had been altered symbolically. This interpretation would certainly not result in any problems for an Anglican today. He was on less secure ground when it came to his adherence to the theory of predestination, which denied the effectiveness of free will and works as a means to salvation. His attitude toward transubstantiation was in opposition to the normative theological position of his day.

Those who took up Wyclif's cause in the form of Wyclifism extended his criticisms of the church beyond acceptable limits and further complicated matters by failing to enunciate any distinct doctrine of their own to replace the one they were so busy attempting to knock down. Thus Wyclif's ideas moved from what has been described as "tolerable criticism" to "intolerable deviance."

The Lollards also failed to promulgate a distinct statement of their beliefs, but a summary of some of their tenets will do much to clarify their unpopularity with the institutional church.

The Lollards accepted remanence in their eucharistic doctrine. They also favored the doctrine of predestination. They were in favor of the promulgation of scripture in the vernacular. The rest of the Lollards' beliefs can best be described by listing what they opposed: payment for prayers, pilgrimages, the efficacy of saints, priestly celibacy, female vows of chastity, "unnecessary crafts" in churches, the intercession of images (icons and statues), the union of secular and ecclesiastical lordship, all forms of church property, and prayers for the dead. They were profoundly anticlerical and believed in the priesthood of all believers. Such a movement would obviously appeal to lay persons, especially those who felt downtrodden by the social and economic structure of the times. The Lollards were therefore blamed for the Peasants' Rebellion, although there seems to be no justification for this accusation. They were, however, at the heart of Sir John Oldcastle's revolt in 1414. This Lollard sympathizer planned an uprising from his prison cell, from which he escaped with the intention of kidnapping members of the royal family. His plot failed miserably but provided an opportunity for ruthless suppression of the Lollard movement, which from this time lost the support of the gentry and went underground. The movement surfaced on occasion in various Lollard trials, including those held in Norwich in the 1420s.

In their adherence to the theory of the priesthood of all believers, the Lollards were early advocates of the role of women, and there are those who claim that Julian herself was subject to this movement. Her deep commitment to the institutional church and her frequent admonitions to her readers to stay loyal to Mother Church make this claim unlikely, although she did share some of the Lollards' criticisms of the church. A study of the summary of their beliefs shows that much of their criticism would have to be seen as valid in the light of what we accept as orthodox belief today. That we, Julian and the Lollards should agree in identification of some of the church's problems does not, however, turn us or Julian into Lollards, any more than Richard Caistor's suggestion that the church's property belongs to the poor makes him a card-carrying Lollard, even though there were those who accused him of just that.

What was the response of the institutional church to Lollardy? Little action was taken prior to 1380, except for excommunication and summons before the ecclesiastical authorities. After 1382 heretics became liable to arrest. From 1388, the secular courts began to assume a greater role in the process of discovery and imprisonment. In 1397 pressure had increased sufficiently, that demands were made for the death penalty, and in 1401 the statute *De Heretico Comburendo*, by which proven heretics were to be burned at the stake, came into force. Also from about 1388, all religious books in the vernacular came under suspicion, which is one reason that Julian's *Revelations* may not have received widespread circulation at the time of her writing of the Longer Version, at about 1393. In spite of the rigor with which the Lollards were eventually suppressed, the church, by and large, was more concerned with the saving of the heretic's individual soul than the destruction of lives.

Norwich itself seems to have suffered little from heresy during the fourteenth century, and there is no evidence of continuing activity by the Lollards in this city. No one from Norwich is known to have participated in Oldcastle's uprising of 1414. Norman Tanner suggests that the health of the church in Norwich at this time left Lollardy as an unattractive and superfluous alternative:

An important reason for the lack of interest in Lollardy was that the religion provided by the local Church was sufficiently rich and varied, and sufficiently tolerant towards what might be called the left wing of orthodoxy, as to cater for the tastes of most citizens (Tanner, p.166).

I would add the suggestion that the "high church" tradition in Norwich, already noted, and the rich liturgical practice associated with that tradition, coupled with the perceived essential role of the ordained priesthood in the celebration of the mass, would mitigate against any support for a movement that was "low church" and protestant and that denied the role of the ordained clergy. In addition, then as now, Norwich displayed a consistent conservatism in most areas of both social and religious change, favoring a slow, reactive response to any association with the vanguard of change in matters of social structure and faith.

If Julian lived into the 1420s, which is probable, her anchorhold was located close to the Lollards' Pit in Norwich, where those convicted of Lollardy were burned. The evidence does not, however, suggest that a large number of citizens of Norwich met this fate; theirs was a city where heresy never became a major concern.

The Church in Transition

The fourteenth century witnessed a blossoming of religious expression in which the laity were playing an increasing role. As has been suggested, the city of Norwich offered an unusual diversity of opportunities for citizens to find religous affiliations to suit each one's individual spiritual taste. The growth of the power of the monarchy and the great increase in the control exercised by the secular city government saw the church beginning to lose its control over the lives of individuals just as it had reached its most ubiquitous infiltration into every element of society. The church had perhaps expanded so far beyond its appropriate border that change or reformation became as necessary as it was inevitable. Norwich at this time, therefore, was the setting for two movements that were eventually to clash and lead to the Reformation. On the one hand, there was a rapid and unusual growth of new institutions, which at least started with the intention of providing religious activities. On the other hand, the traditional role of the church was beginning to be challenged and the laity were asserting a greater proportion of control and authority over the activities of the church. Humanism was beginning to infiltrate the thought of the day. Although it began as a strictly Christian humanism, the germ of this philosophy, once firmly in place, was to expand until the course of history would change and the church would lose much of its power, soon after it appeared to reach its apex.

Although many were founded in the thirteenth century, the guilds and pious confraternities of Norwich reached their preeminence in the second half of the fourteenth and the first half of the fifteenth centuries. By the middle of the fifteenth century there were approximately fifty such bodies in Norwich. In 1389 nineteen guilds and confraternities were registered in Norwich, as compared with thirty in Lincoln, forty-one in London, and the amazing total of fifty-one in Lynn. The chief purpose of these organizations was originally religious, with emphasis on fraternity and charity between members. It was not long, however, before the religious purpose of the craft guilds, while maintained, took second place to the economic and political control of the specific trades that the guilds represented. The pious confraternities remained just that, with the possible exception of the Corpus Christi confraternity, whose membership was restricted to priests, both beneficed and unbeneficed. The activities of this organization had all the appearance of a craft guild for priests.

Craft guilds were responsible for guild days and annual masses, which were not held in the parish churches but most often at the cathedral, thus demonstrating that the multiplicity of churches in Norwich is not explained by the large number of craft guilds, because they were not guild churches. The founding of churches may well have been the result of the competitive spirit between successful and wealthy merchant families, but this competition was over by the time with which we are concerned. Most of the craft guilds offered financial assistance to those members in need of support and provided burial and help with funeral costs for their own. The growth of the guild movement led initially to an expansion in religious activities, and although this expansion enhanced the role of the laity in the life of the church, it should be borne in mind that many of these activities required the offices of a priest. The guilds in this way provided employment for both beneficed and unbeneficed clergy.

The pious confraternities, with the exception of Corpus Christi already noted, were not related to crafts or trades, but were either connected to parishes or to religious houses, non-parochial churches, and colleges. Among the most active were the Confraternity of the Annunciation of St. Mary, which was founded to support the College of St. Mary in the Fields; Corpus

Christi, restricted to priests; and St. George's Confraternity, which we have already encountered in its role of providing the depiction of St. George and the dragon in the annual procession honoring their patron saint. Founded in 1385, this confraternity from its inception held close ties to the government of the city. It received a Royal Charter in 1417, giving it a clear superiority over the other confraternities, and in 1452 its activities were actually united into the city government's organization.

Responsibility for processions and the production of mystery plays, in conjunction with annual masses, became the focal point of these societies. Yet lest we be encouraged to believe that these confraternities were overburdened with religious intent and pietistic seriousness, we should take note that the annual feast was held to be every bit as important as the mass or the procession. We should also recognize that the formal records of the activities of the confraternities were likely to contain greater emphasis on their religious endeavors than on their more extravagant indulgence in bacchanalian celebration.

Devotion to the saints increased during this period, encouraged officially by the church. Due honor was to be accorded the persons of the Trinity, a reminder to the faithful in an age in which devotion to Our Lady was on the increase, together with a strong Christology that may have left the first and third persons of the Trinity in danger of neglect. Julian's theology is strongly Trinitarian in impact, possibly a reaction to this tendency, and Julian is strong in her suggestion that praying directly to God is to be preferred over what she describes as prayer "by means," or prayer invoking the mediation of the saints.

Pilgrimages were immensely popular, as any reader of Chaucer's *Canterbury Tales* could surmise. East Anglia boasted some twenty shrines, of which Our Lady of Walsingham survives and provides a prime example, still held in active veneration. Norwich was an important center for pilgrimages, and it was on the occasion of one such pilgrimage to "offer at the Trinity" (the cathedral) that Margery Kempe was afforded the opportunity to meet Julian at her anchorhold.

Crusades were still regarded as appropriate means of expressing one's devotion to the church, although by this time they were less sure in their purpose, the subject of attack ceasing to be the "infidel hoardes" and becoming fellow Christians with whom the crusader disagreed. The crusades of both Henry Despenser, bishop of Norwich, and of John of Gaunt in Castille both exploited the papal rivalries engendered by the Great Schism.

Piety had reached an elaborate stage in which accessories were numerous, varying from the major investment in a private chapel (of which few were evident in Norwich with its superfluity of parish churches) to a proliferation of devotional objects, including rosaries, images of saints, rings, and relics—these last the subject of frequent abuse and notorious in Chaucer's wonderful description of the Pardoner.

Masses for the dead were considered an important form of assistance to their passage through purgatory, their value being solemnly proclaimed in a creed prepared by Pope Clement IV for Emperor Michael VIII Palaeologus and recited in the emperor's name at the Council of Lyons in 1274:

> We believe that the intercessions of the faithful who are living help to relieve their pains (i.e., of the souls in Purgatory), that is to say Masses, prayers, alms and other works of piety, which have customarily been performed by the faithful, on behalf of others of the faithful, according to the approved practices of the church (Tanner, p. 92).

Some forty perpetual chantries were initiated in Norwich after 1369, originating from five principal sources: craft guilds and pious confraternities, bishops, other clerics from the city, East Anglian members of the gentry, and prominent laymen of Norwich. When perpetual chantries proved beyond the means of the testator, annual masses for a period of months or years or prayers for the dead were provided. The annual masses would frequently occur for a period of up to four years. A few left instructions for a priest to be paid to journey to Rome, to intercede on the deceased's behalf.

Most of these developments in pietistic practice demonstrate a continuing growth in concern for the soul's passage through purgatory, a belief that prayer was an effective instrument toward relief from such torment, and a sense that the church did provide valuable services, especially the mass, whose greatest effectiveness may well be posthumous. This piety raised the question of the efficacy of one mass as compared with a multiplicity of masses. If the effect of the mass was complete on one occasion, wherein lay the necessity for repetition? The response to this dilemma, in what might be seen as an example of Anglican compromise, was that while one mass was as effective as many, the Church would not stand in the way of the wealthy seeking a little additional insurance by providing employment for chantry priests and mass priests in perpetuity.

As mentioned earlier, the growth of elaborate pietism in the fourteenth century was accompanied by the first signs of the humanist movement, a tension that we will encounter throughout Julian's theology.

R.N. Swanson provides an analysis of this force at work:

> Drawing on a classic concern with the restoration of the pristine church, and preferring the doctrines of the Patristics to later theologians, the intellectual movement also shared in the general concern for moral reform and some of the ideas of the *devotio moderna*. Internationally, its supreme exponent was Erasmus. . . . Christian humanism cannot be divorced from preceding movements. For all its Christocentricity and laicizing near-mysticism, Christian humanism was firmly linked to earlier spiritual trends. . . . Although railing against ecclesiastical abuses, and demanding the restoration of a purified church, it did not negate late medieval spirituality. In many ways, indeed, it seems to represent its logical culmination (Swanson, pp. 347–48).

Thus, the logical direction in which both the piety and the nascent humanism of the late Middle Ages were to lead was that movement which had already begun throughout Europe and which was to reach England. There the English Reformation was to absorb parts of the several distinct reform movements on the Continent and amalgamate them into the peculiar hybrid that gave us the Church of England as we still know it. Technically, the English Reformation is dated from 1529, with complete separation from Rome effective by 1536, but it can be persuasively argued that the Reformation can trace its roots to the very period in which Julian flourished.

4

Anchorites in the Late Middle Ages

The word "anchorite" is derived from the Greek *anachoretes*, which means "withdrawn from the world." In addition to the way of life connoted by this term, there is a secondary association with the anchoring of a ship, suggesting that the anchorite was anchored beneath the church in a commitment to stability, which formed part of the anchorite's vows. The term *anchoress*, applied to Julian, is merely the female form of the word *anchorite*, which is used to describe the vocation generically, irrespective of the gender of the one described. Anchorites are also described by the Latin words *inclusus/inclusa* and *reclusus/reclusa*, and the English also referred to male anchorites as "ankers." To this day, there are still individuals who choose to live a life apart, in hermitages, within enclosed orders, or as recluses. The actual order of anchorite was suppressed at the time of the Dissolution of the Monasteries in the sixteenth century.

Anchorites were not necessarily members of religious orders, though some took their vows as anchorites in addition to regular monastic vows. The vocation required episcopal permission, following rigorous examination by one appointed by the bishop, and anchorites served their vocation under the direction and supervision of the diocesan bishop. Anchorites were supposed to be supported by the alms of the parish community to which they were attached.

The rite of enclosure for the anchorite made a dramatic statement as to the serious nature of the commitment, declaring the anchorite dead to the world. This was emphasized by the celebration of a requiem mass for the anchorite, by the burial of the anchorite into his or her anchorhold with the sprinkling of earth, and by the bolting of the entrance to the cell, whose prisonlike qualities included its size, approximately twelve feet square, and the sparseness of the prescribed furnishings. The ceremony of enclosure, which survives in the Sarum Rite, was preceded by a full confession of sins and the consumption of only bread and water during the twenty-four hours before the enclosure. The preceding night was passed in vigil. Fourteen psalms, selected for their penitential quality, were chosen for the liturgy and were part of the ministry of the Word which preceded the mass. Following the mass, the one to be enclosed made a solemn profession, and the simple habit was blessed and sprinkled with holy water. The professed then prostrated him- or herself. Leaving the church, the officiants and the anchorite formed a solemn procession and proceeded to the anchorhold as a litany was chanted. The anchorhold was blessed; the bishop led the anchorite into the cell by the hand and then left, closing the door, which the rubric commands should be "firmly enclosed from without."

We do not know precisely to which rule the quite large number of anchorites in Norwich were bound, but for the purposes of this study, we can assume that it would have borne a marked similarity to the *Ancrene Riwle*, the rule proposed by an anonymous author to three women who intended to pursue vocations as anchoresses in the thirteenth century. The instructions of this rule coincide with much that can be learned concerning Julian's way of life as it emerges from her *Revelations*, our only immediate source on the particular nature of her discipline. I will therefore devote considerable time to this remarkable work, which probably formed a regular element in Julian's own reading.

I am indebted to Robert W. Ackerman and Roger Dahood for much of the information covering the *Ancrene Riwle*, to be found in their *Ancrene Riwle: Introduction and Part I*. The English text may be found in E.J. Dobson, *The English Text of the Ancrene Riwle, B.M.Cotton MS Cleopatra, C. VI*, and a prime study of the *Riwle* was made by M.B. Salu, *The Ancrene Riwle*.

What follows is a summary of the findings of this scholarship, to give the reader an understanding of the way of life Julian chose for herself sometime after her visions in 1373.

The Ancrene Riwle

The author of the *Ancrene Riwle*—or the *Ancrene Wisse*, as it is sometimes called—describes two rules that govern the religious life, the *inner*, or "lady" rule, and the *outer*, or "handmaid" rule. The former concerns the heart, which must be kept "right" in its quest for God, and the latter, which pertains to the body and the exterior life, being man-made, is destined to serve the inner rule.

The anchoress was to take three solemn vows, the violation of which amounted to a mortal sin: the vow of obedience, especially to one's bishop or other superior; the vow of chastity; and the vow of stability of abode. Charity, observance of the Ten Commandments, confession, penitence, and other matters that we might expect to form part of the vows were not included, since they are decreed by God and not subject to the taking of any vow. If asked to which order she belonged, a question that would have been prevalent in a society permeated with many different religious orders and confraternities, the anchoress was to reply that she was a member of the order of St. James, the patron saint of anchorites.

The *Ancrene Riwle* is presented in eight parts or "distinctions":

I. Devotions

Upon awakening, the anchoress was to cross herself, and say the *In Nomine Patris*, and the *Veni, Creator Spiritus*. She was then to recite the *Pater Noster* while dressing. She was then to say prayers in memory of the five wounds of Christ and to venerate the relics on each of her several altars. She would then begin to recite the offices, which will be listed later. The anchoress was encouraged to recite English prayers in her private devotions. As she observed the mass through her "squint," or small window, which gave a view from her cell of the high altar of the church, at the elevation of the Host, the anchoress was to say a series of prayers, offer the kiss of peace (an ancient practice recently returned to the liturgy amid mixed reviews), and forget all the world and extend her love to the Savior. At midday, she was to meditate on the cross. She was to kneel in prayer before and after meals. At all costs, she was to avoid idleness, listen to the priest's hours, and to say grace at meals.

II. The Five Senses

The five senses are the guardians of the heart, which can be a wild creature much in need of control and discipline. In the matter of sight, the anchoress should keep her parlor window closed, never opening it for a man, and only on occasions of necessity to a woman. The small window was hung with three layers of thick cloth, two black and one white. The two black layers were to have a cross-shaped opening cut into them, and the white layer was to remain whole and be placed between the two black layers. The result was a white cross on a black background. Thus only a minimal amount of light could pass through, but the sound of a voice was readily heard.

As far as sound or speech was concerned, the anchoress must be controlled in speech, not like a "cackling hen." She was not permitted to converse through her squint, which was to be reserved strictly for her observation of the mass and the other offices. She was to maintain silence at meals, and any guests were to be entertained on her behalf by her servant or servants. She was to model herself on Our Lady, who was typified as one who spoke seldom.

The anchoress's ears should be stopped against all idle and evil talk. Backbiters and flatterers were to be avoided. One of the obvious risks of the vow of stability would have been the presumed availability of the anchoress to everyone in the neighborhood with time to pass in idle chat and gossip. Any active parish clergy know the regular customer with time on his or her hands and a well-developed curiosity about any items of interest in the lives of others.

The *Riwle* suggests that the sins of the eyes are effectively covered in the scriptures and by the early Fathers, St. Gregory being a good example.

With regard to the sense of smell, the anchoress is told that the devil can make something good smell bad and something evil smell ravishing. She is instructed that a genuine holy smell appeals to the heart more than to the nose. Incense was in general use in Norwich; evidence for this is found in the inventory for St. Peter Mancroft, already quoted as the source of elaborate priestly vestments for processions. Given the level of personal and public hygiene, also mentioned earlier, the need for incense went far beyond personal, liturgical, stylistic preference and continued to perform its practical function, which originated in temple worship, replete with the odors associated with animal sacrifice. The anchoress was also encouraged to make full use of holy water and the sign of the cross in seeking to avoid deceptions.

Christ's five wounds were seen to provide healing blood for the sins of the five senses. Christ's perfect steadfastness was a reminder that the life of the soul may be preserved intact only through proper custody and control of these senses.

III. David's Comparison of Himself to the Birds in the Psalter

The heart of the anchoress was to grow in humility. The references to birds in the psalter offer examples of this desired humility, which the anchoress would do well to imitate. She is reminded of the pelican, who, out of anger, slew her own young. But the pelican's austerity keeps her light in weight, allowing her to soar into the air. The anchoress was to keep herself trim, so that she might soar spiritually and avoid the fate of the overweight and land-bound ostrich. The anchoress must learn to live content in a hard, thorny nest, her anchorhold. As the raven gathers food by night, so the anchoress was to gather the fruits of spiritual contemplation through the night. She was to be as watchful as a sparrow. The author examines eight reasons for her remaining ever vigilant and eight further reasons for her fleeing into solitude, among which fear of the devil features prominently. The anchoress should say her prayers by herself, in emulation of the lone sparrow and she should not forget that just as the sparrow is subject to falling sickness, so is the anchoress always subject to temptation. These delightful ornithological parables, while possibly lacking scientific authenticity, illustrate the warmth and humanity that pervade the *Ancrene Riwle*, and demonstrate a profound knowledge of the human intellect, which is far more likely to remember an illustrated point than a long list of prescriptive orders and regulations. That Christ taught in parables, and that sermon illustrations are recalled long after the rest of the sermon is forgotten, are endorsements of the method espoused by the writer of the *Ancrene Riwle*.

IV. Fleshy and Spiritual Temptations

The anchoress is warned that one of the greatest perils is that encountered when one feels no temptation. Two types of temptation are described, not surprisingly "inner" and "outer." The outer temptations are subdivided as incurring either external or internal discomforts. External discomforts include illness, shame, misfortune, and bodily harm. Internal outer discomforts are such as pain of the heart and anger. These can be assuaged by external comforts, as in bodily health and sufficient food, drink, and clothing; or by internal comforts, such as happiness at praise received or at being loved more than another. Patience is seen as the most effective weapon against these outer temptations.

Inner temptations are also twofold, the bodily and the spiritual. These are typified by the Seven Capital Sins and their "vile progeny," characterized by appropriate animals, as follows:

Bodily			Spiritual		
Lechery	—	Scorpion	Pride	—	Lion
Gluttony	—	Sow	Envy	—	Adder
Sloth	—	Bear	Wrath	—	Unicorn
			Avarice	—	Fox

The anchoress is reminded that each of these animals is capable of bearing many young cubs. She is warned that temptation grows more, not less, difficult with time. There are four degrees of temptation: strong, weak, open, and concealed. Temptation in its concealed form is regarded as the most pernicious. For example, the devil can urge the anchoress to such extremes of abstinence that her soul will die as a result of her bodily deprivations. In this, as in so many of the instructions in the *Ancrene Riwle*, one is struck by the resonableness of the tone and the determination to prevent excessive pietism and fanatic obsession in surroundings where these must have remained constant risks. As the writer explains, the higher the tower, the stronger the wind. The anchoress must imagine God to be playing with her as a mother plays with her child. Active resistance to the devil injures him a hundredfold, and no one will be saved, as St. Paul reminds us, except by struggling against temptation. The anchoress is put in mind of additional medicines to be prescribed against the disease of temptation: meditation, anguished prayer, reading, fasting, humility, and magnaminity. With faith, the anchoress may "laugh the old ape, the devil, to scorn."

Several further antidotes to sin are described. To guard against pride, the anchoress is to think how humble God made himself in the Virgin's womb; against wrath, she must think of peace between man and man, God and man, and man and angel; against sloth, she must recall how busy Christ was during his ministry on earth. Remedies are suggested: for pride, humility; for envy, love of fellow men; for wrath, patience; for sloth, reading, work, or spiritual comfort; and for avarice, contempt for worldly things. The dog of hell was to be beaten back by the crucifix of faith, not only metaphorically but literally. It is worth noting that Julian was brought a crucifix to gaze on during the temptations she encountered as part of her visionary experience. Whenever she felt the growth of excessive love for worldly things, the anchoress should tread on the serpent's head at its first appearance, for much may grow from little; from one spark may come a raging fire.

V. Confession

The author of the *Ancrene Riwle* names six "powers" and six-teen "qualities" of confession. He remains consistent in his strongly anthropomorphic treatment of evil in the form of the devil here as throughout the work. Among its powers, confession destroys the devil's power by hacking off his head and dispersing his army, an action compared to Judith's decapitation of Holofernes. Confession restores to the penitent anchoress her loss by washing out her sins and making her once again a child of God. Among its qualities, confession must be accusatory, bitter with sorrow, whole, naked, frequent, speedy, humble, shame-faced, and fearful. St. Augustine's guidance is invoked. Reason should be man's judge, memory his accuser, and conscience a witness against him. Fear should bind him against further sin. During confession, the anchoress is to reveal six "circumstances": the identity of any other person involved in the confessed sin, the place, the time, the manner, the frequency, and the cause of the sin. Nine reasons for hastening to confession are then sup-plied, including the possibility that death or debilitating disease might intervene before the sinner has had an opportunity to con-fess, leaving her liable to the possibility of meeting her maker unshriven, a state considered to have dreadful circumstances in an age preoccupied with death, purgatory, and the possibility of everlasting damnation. The anchoress's confession was to be pru-dent, truthful, and voluntary, and it should be concerned with the anchoress's own sins, as opposed to the sins of others with which she might have become acquainted. She was instructed to confess in particular the following catalogue of sins: pride, haughty heart, envy, wrath, sloth, idle words, gluttony, and excessive abstinence. In addition, confession was required fol-lowing instances in which the anchoress had said the hours badly. It was suggested that atonement for minor faults should be sought by the immediate action of falling before the altar in the form of a cross and saying "mea culpa." In the midst of this awe-inspiring list of potential faults, the mere examination of which produces guilt in the reader, we continue to see evidence of moderation, as in the listing of "excessive abstinence" as a sin.

VI. *Penance*

The author defines three kinds of God's chosen on this earth: those who are like good pilgrims, those who imitate the dead, and those who hang themselves voluntarily on the cross of Jesus. The first, the good pilgrims, travel the course they have been set, curbing their worldly appetites. The second, as with the dead, find their lives hidden with Christ. The third, bound on the cross of Christ, reap joy and honor as the reward gained for them by Christ in his shame and torment. The writer qualifies these three kinds as being good, better, and best respectively, and suggests that the true anchoress combines all three as a pilgrim, dead to the world, accepting the martyrdom that Christ offers her. Julian not only prayed for such qualities, but felt herself to be physically included in Christ's passion and death. It is through suffering that the anchoress, and indeed we ourselves, come to reign with Christ. As Ackerman and Dahood state it:

> One asks, "What good do I do for God by my torments?" But, as St. Ailred wrote to his sister, one may attain purity only in two ways. One is through mortification of the body by fasting, vigils, discipline and great labor. The other is through the virtues: devotion, compassion, love, humility and such (Ackerman and Dahood, p. 25).

These virtues are pervasive in Julian's theology, as we shall see. The author of the *Ancrene Riwle* compares Christ to a recluse, and sees Mary's womb and the stone sepulchre as the equivalents of Christ's anchorhold.

Once again, in treating the subject of penance, the counselor advises the anchoress not to overdo her mortification.

VII. *Cleanness of Heart and the Love of Christ*

The anchoress is reminded that all the physical hardships in the world are nothing compared with the love that Paul describes in 1 Corinthians 13, a love which cleanses and brightens the heart. It does not matter how greatly one mortifies the flesh or how deeply one is committed to almsgiving, if the love of God and fellow creature is absent. Above all, the anchoress is to strive for a pure heart, to love and desire nothing but God, for "God deserves our love, for he gave us the world, and Christ loved the Church, and sacrificed his life for it" (Ackerman and Dahood, p.25).

The writer then tells the story of a lady surrounded by her foes in her earthly castle. She ignores the attentions of a king who attempts to court her. The king is then slain. The question is whether the lady is capable of loving the king in death, after his sacrifice of himself. In this parable the king is Christ and the lady is the human soul. The death of the king reveals the strength of his love. The anchoress is then instructed in the four varieties of earthly love: that between friends, that between man and woman, that between mother and child, and that between body and soul. Christ's love for his spouse, the church, surpasses all four of these loves. Sin, idleness, and a sour heart quench the love of the Lord, as urine, sand, and vinegar quench Greek fire. In sum, the anchoress should stretch forth her love to Jesus.

VIII. The Outer Rule

Whereas the laity were mandated to receive communion at least once a year, the anchoress was to receive it fifteen times a year, including several stipulated feast days. In preparation for this, the anchoress should be shriven and take discipline, which should be self-administered. If for any reason it was impossible to receive communion on a prescribed day, as in the absence of a priest, the anchoress was to take communion on the following Sunday. From Easter until the Feast of the Exaltation of the Holy Cross, on September 14, she was to eat two meals daily except Fridays, Ember Days, and a few other fast days. For the rest of the year, one meal a day was deemed sufficient. Fish and fat were to be consumed only by the very weak or ill. The anchoress was encouraged to drink little, but to eat as many vegetables as she wished. Fasting was to be accomplished only on bread and water, and then only with the permission of her superior. She was forbidden to eat with guests. The author observes that he has often heard of the dead speaking to the living, but never has he heard of the dead eating with the living, and the anchoress is, after all, supposed to be dead to the world. I cannot help wondering what the author of the *Ancrene Riwle* made of Christ's meal with the disciples at Emmaus, not to mention a consideration of Christ's presence in the eucharist, but his thrust is clearly aimed at eliminating unseemly public eating with the laity. Further, the anchoress should refrain from entertaining others, from encouraging strangers to visit, and from distributing alms too lavishly. She should play the quiet, meditative role of Mary rather than undertake the constant activities of Martha. She was, however, permitted to give meals to the women and children who come to work for her, but must never permit any man to eat in her presence. She was to accept whatever she needs from good friends, but must be careful to avoid gaining a reputation as a "gathering anchoress."

The anchoress was prohibited from keeping any animals, with the exception of a cat, which was to be kept for utilitarian purposes. Cows were specifically proscribed. The anchoress was to avoid all business transactions and is warned against keeping the possessions of others in her cell. The possibility of having an anchoress permanently on watch over valuables must have appealed to many parishioners. One imagines someone saying to a friendly anchoress, "Could you just keep an eye on my jewelry while I go away on a pilgrimage?"

In her dress, the anchoress is commanded to wear plain, warm, well-made garments, it being of no consequence whether they are white or black (indicating that any other colors would be frowned upon). No linen was to be worn, except of the coarsest kind, next to the flesh. She was to sleep in belted gowns and should refrain from donning anything made of iron, hair, or hedgehog skin—a hint of some of the extremes of mortification that must have been attempted. Along similar lines, the anchoress should not beat herself with a leaded whip or briar, nor should she draw blood in taking discipline, except with her confessor's express permission. We are reminded that flagellation was common practice as a form of penance in this time. The anchoress need not wear a wimple, but should at least wear cap and veil in the presence of others. Rings, brooches, and gloves were specifically forbidden.

By way of suitable occupational therapy, the anchoress was encouraged to sew church vestments and clothing for the destitute, but was not to accept commissions for fancy purses nor should such be distributed as gifts. No material goods were to be either given or received without the permission of the confessor. Idleness must be avoided at all cost. Anchoresses were not to offer instruction to young girls, a task which they were presumably asked to perform frequently. They were permitted to delegate this worthy task to one of their handmaidens.

Anchoresses were to have their hair cut regularly to lighten their heads and were to be bled for their health's sake on occasion. Following this normative medical procedure of the times, the anchoress was warned to avoid overtaxing herself for the three days thereafter.

As far as securing provisions was concerned, one of the two suggested servants was to do the shopping, but in carrying out this menial task, she was to be plainly dressed and to be observed saying her prayers as she went about her business. The servants were warned strictly to avoid turning these shopping trips into opportunities for the exchange of the latest gossip. The instructions to the servants were to be read to them once a week until they showed clear signs that they had absorbed them and could then abide by them.

Hardly surprisingly, the anchoress is encouraged to read from the *Ancrene Riwle* daily. The author expresses the hope that it will prove helpful through God's grace, and states that he would rather undertake a journey to Rome than have to undertake the writing of the *Riwle* a second time. He commands the anchoresses to greet Our Lady with an *Ave*, as often as they read the *Ancrene Riwle*, on behalf of him who labored over it. The whole book is permeated with the gentleness, moderation, and warmth of its author and offers an unique window into the life and times in which it was created. It is likely that Julian followed the *Riwle* closely.

Devotions of an Anchoress

Given the Benedictine character of both the cathedral and the Carrow Priory, which held the patronage of St. Julian's, it is almost certain that Julian's devotions would have followed those suggested within the *Ancrene Riwle*, which could be described as "modified Benedictine rule." The *Opus Dei* or *Opus Divinum*, or the Hours, were the prime obligation of the monastic day, along with the *Lectio Divina*, consisting of spiritual or theological reading, and the *Opus Manuum*, which covered manual work in the fields or elsewhere, as in the institutional bakery. As ordained by the psalms, official worship was to take place seven times a day and once at night. The names of the offices were derived from Roman divisions of the day. Vespers in the late afternoon was commonly considered the first expression within the liturgical day, but modern interpretation will be better served if we start with the first devotional action of the early morning, as we set forth a typical day of devotion for the anchoress. I am indebted to Ackerman and Dahood (pp. 37–38) for this reconstruction of an anchoress's "Horarium" (or Hours).

The Anchoress's Horarium

3:00 – 5:00 A.M.	Preliminary devotions and prayers
	Matins and lauds of Our Lady
	Dirige (matins and lauds of the Office of the Dead)
	Suffrages and Commendation
	Litany of the Saints (daily except Sundays)
	Lauds of the Holy Ghost (optional)
5:00 – 6:00 A.M.	Listen to the priest's celebration of the canonical hours when possible
6:00 – 7:00 A.M.	Prime of the Holy Ghost (optional)
	Prime of Our Lady
7:00 – 8:00 A.M.	Preciosa
8:00 – 9:00 A.M.	Terce of the Holy Ghost (optional)
	Terce of Our Lady
9:00 – 10:00 A.M.	Prayers and supplications
	Devotions before the cross
10:00 – 11:00 A.M.	Devotions to Our Lady
	The Seven Penitential Psalms
	The Fifteen Gradual Psalms
11:00 – 12:00 NOON	Mass (communion fifteen times annually)
12:00 – 1:00 P.M.	Sext of the Holy Ghost (optional)
	Sext of Our Lady
	Meal (first meal in summer; only meal on weekdays in winter)
1:00 – 2:00 P.M.	None of the Holy Ghost (optional)
	None of Our Lady
2:00 – 3:00 P.M.	Rest period
3:00 – 5:00 P.M.	Private prayers and meditation
	Reading in psalter, *Ancrene Riwle,* and other edifying works
	Instruction of maidservants
	Work: plain needlework on church vestments or clothing for the poor
	Vespers of the Holy Ghost (optional)
	Vespers of Our Lady
	Placebo (Vespers of the Office of the Dead, omitted before a feast of nine lessons)
	Meal (second meal on Sundays and on weekdays in summer only)
5:00 – 7:00 P.M.	Compline of the Holy Ghost (optional)
	Compline of Our Lady
	Bedtime prayers and devotions.

It is to be noted that devotions to the Holy Ghost were optional, reflecting the concentration on Our Lady and the highly developed Christology of the period, as discussed earlier. Variations occurred according to the different amount of light available in winter and summer. In the eleventh century the various books required—the psalter, antiphonary, hymnal, lectionary, responsorial, Gospels, and book of homilies—were combined into the Breviary, which was portable and contained all that was necessary for the regular saying of the hours, making it possible for monks and friars to maintain their spiritual discipline even when they were absent from their cloisters. The formalization of routine, daily prayer by the secular clergy, now so much a part of the Anglican tradition, was to develop later than the period with which we are involved. The Sarum Use, that which was employed at Salisbury, was in widespread acceptance throughout the country. Votive offices, reflecting the growing popularity of the cult of saints, were added to the Breviary. Neither the potential anchoresses, addressed by the author of the Ancrene Riwle, nor Julian appear to have had monastic experience, and would thus have made use of a Book of Hours in English. "Prymers," an early form of the Book of Common Prayer, appeared first in Julian's century. The Office of Our Lady was substituted for the monastic office in the rule for the anchoress.

Reading the detail of the Horarium, we get the impression that the poor anchoress must have spent her entire day kneeling at prayer. This would be an exaggeration, since the offices were designed to be short but frequent, constantly interrupting the day in order to prevent idleness or distraction from the principal purpose of the vocation. In broad terms, the offices enumerated above would have taken the anchoress about four hours to complete. This would have left plenty of time for counseling and other ministrations, as well as several hours for silent contemplation, a period in which Julian must have engaged in contemplation of her original visions, a reexamination which she herself describes as lasting for twenty years.

The evidence suggests that Julian was a particularly conscientious adherent to both her rule and her hours, however close to the Ancrene Riwle and the Horarium they may or may not have been. The question arises as to the potential gulf between theory and practice. Blomefield, in his history of Norfolk, quotes Becon's Reliques of Rome, folio 312, in an account of abuse among anchorites indicating that some anchorites failed to maintain the high standards to which they were called.

We have now had an opportunity to gain some insight into the life of the anchoress, both as it was intended to be lived and when it had fallen prey to the temptations of the secular world. Given the evidence, Julian was an exemplary follower of such rule as was available to her. As the author of the *Ancrene Riwle* suggests, the anchoress is encouraged toward moderation within her strict discipline, and we would be wrong to conjure up visions of excessive masochism. The fact that the anchoress was expected to be provided with one or more servants reinforces the image of a reasonable manner of life. It is also likely that Julian came from a well-to-do background, as from possibly a wealthy merchant family, and having two servants, was well provided for, so that we should not suppose a life of abject poverty. We next turn to the literary influences that may have been available to an anchoress in her time, within the context of the church in Norwich that has earlier been described.

5

Julian's Sources

Literature of the Fourteenth Century and Other Influences

Julian is counted as one of the four great mystical writers of the fourteenth century, taking her place alongside Richard Rolle, Walter Hilton, and the anonymous author of *The Cloud of Unknowing*. The extent to which Julian was influenced by any or all of these her contemporaries is hard to quantify, and we cannot know either the extent to which Julian influenced them. We can say with confidence that all four were writing in approximately the same period, that they were concerned with similar issues, and that all must surely refect the theology and piety of that period. A common thread of faith and love for God runs through all these works, and such similarities as do occur allow us to at least posit that these writers knew of each other's existence, even if they had not read them fully.

Julian's dependence on biblical passages permeates the *Revelations*, and we will study this source in a separate section. Of those influences which appear to have had an effect on her writing and which predate her, the two most significant for our purposes were Augustine and Anselm.

Julian shared Augustine's vision of the Trinity, in which God the Father is power, God the Son is wisdom, and God the Holy Spirit is goodness or love—the whole Trinity being united in our creation and delighting in it, as Julian expresses it:

> And so in our making, God almighty is our loving Father, and God all wisdom is our loving mother, with the love and goodness of the Holy Spirit, which is all one God, one Lord (CW, p.293; ET, pp. 582-83).

The mothering role of Christ reoccurs in the following passage:

Our Father wills, our Mother works, our good Lord the Holy
Spirit confirms. And therefore it is our part to love our God in
whom we have our being, reverently thanking and praising
him for our creation, mightily praying to our Mother for
mercy and pity, and to our Lord the Holy Spirit for help and
grace. For in these three is all our life (CW, p.296; ET, pp.
591-92).

Julian's sense of our createdness in God and God's presence
within us finds solid reflection in Augustine's words:

How shall I call upon my God, my God and my Lord, since in
truth, when I call upon him, I call him into myself? . . . O Lord
my God, is there anything in me that can contain you? In
truth, can heaven and earth, which you have made and in
which you have made me, contain you? Or because without
you whatever is would not be, does it hold that whatever
exists contains you? I would not be, I would in no wise be,
unless you were in me. Or rather, I would not be unless I were
in you, "from whom, by whom and in whom are all
things" . . . To what place do I call you, since I am in you?"
(Ryan, trans., *Confessions* I.2).

Julian agrees with Augustine in that no matter how far we may
distance ourselves from God in our consciousness and our
behavior, our essential substance with God is retained.

Julian's debt to Anselm appears to be considerable. Much has
been made of Julian's contribution to current theology in terms of
her perception of the feminine, mothering role of Christ, a role
which we will study in greater depth when we review her theology
in detail. In terms of potential literary sources, it would be hard to
conceive that Julian did not know Anselm's *Prayer to St. Paul*:

And you, Jesus, are you not also a mother?
Are you not the mother who, like a hen,
Gathers her chickens under her wings?
Truly, Lord, you are a mother,
For both they who are in labour
And they who are brought forth
Are accepted by you . . .

(Ward, p. 153)

The metaphor of Christ as the mother hen comes from our

Lord's description of himself in Matthew 23:37, but the emphasis on this element of Christ's nature, seen in Anselm, is taken to new levels by Julian in her *Revelations*.

To proceed in approximately chronological order, the next work that may well have had a formative effect on Julian is that early masterpiece of English writing, the *Ancrene Riwle*, from the early thirteenth century, which is covered in considerable detail in the section regarding the role of the anchoress in the church in Norwich during Julian's time. It again seems highly likely that those who were responsible as Julian's superiors would have made extensive use of this work in devising her personal rule. They may well have insisted upon her reading this work regularly as part of her devotional discipline, although she makes no direct reference to this or any other devotional work in the text of her *Revelations*.

John Wyclif's contribution to the church in this period has already been discussed in the section describing the state of the church at the time, and it may also be reasonable to consider him in connection with Julian's sources. Given her lack of literacy in Latin, it seems possible, if not probable, that Julian may have taken advantage of Wyclif's translation of the Bible into the English vernacular. Once again, no such credit is bestowed, but Wyclif's lack of popularity with the church authorities would have been sufficient to have made any such acknowledgment ill-advised. The mere possession of a Bible in English was for a while deemed sufficient evidence of connection to Lollardy. Nevertheless, Julian's frequent, if not wholly accurate, quotations from the Bible indicate her possession of an English-text Bible of the period, or at least her access to segments of the Bible in English.

William Langland's classic poem of pilgrimage, *Piers Ploughman*, must surely have been known to Julian. Langland was born at least ten years prior to Julian, and his work must have been readily available to her before the poet's death at about the turn of the century. Langland's threefold vision of Do-Well, Do-Bet, and Do-Best finds many parallels in Julian's frequent three-part approaches to Christian doctrine.

Richard Rolle of Hampole died in 1349, probably of the plague, when Julian was only seven years old, but his work might have proved encouraging to Julian. He wrote his *Fire of Love*, as he stated it, "for the attention of the simple and unlearned who are seeking to love God," an intention that would have found favor with Julian, with her concern for her "even-Christians." Rolle, a mystic and a hermit, wrote several devotional works, with titles such as *The Mending of Life* and *The Form of Perfect Living*, and his work was familiar to Margery Kempe, along with the work of Walter Hilton. It is more than likely that Margery Kempe would have discussed both these writers with Julian during a visit which Margery herself describes as lengthy.

Walter Hilton, best known for his *Scale of Perfection* (also known as *The Ladder of Perfection*), wrote this work to a "ghostly sister in Jesus Christ," who may well have been an anchoress. He was an Augustinian canon of Thurgarton in Nottinghamshire. His works give directions for piety and the overcoming of the Seven Deadly Sins. He appears to have been influenced by Richard Rolle and the author of *The Cloud of Unknowing*, but as has been said before, it is a little dangerous to make any assumptions about who was influencing whom.

It is hard to resist claiming some form of literary relationship between Julian and the greatest writer of her time, Geoffrey Chaucer. Probably born within a year of each other, it seems at least likely that Julian knew of Chaucer's work. However, it should be recalled that Julian wrote her *Short Version of the Revelations* presumably quite soon after they occurred in 1373 and, by her own admission, completed the *Longer Version of the Revelations* some twenty years later, which brings us to 1393. Chaucer only began *The Canterbury Tales* in 1387. It thus seems unlikely that Chaucer had any influence on Julian's writing style, and one must certainly question whether the *Canterbury Tales* would have been considered appropriate reading matter for the anchoress, firmly enclosed in her anchorhold long before this work could have reached her in Norwich. There is, of course, a similarity in the language of the two authors, but this is explained by the fact that both were concerned to make their writngs available to the people in their own language. In the matter of style, Julian's is distinct from Chaucer's, and her claim to be the first female writer in English does not depend on any influence by Chaucer.

If Julian was the first woman writer in English whose work has survived, Margery Kempe can claim to be the first true autobiographer in English, and certainly the first female autobiographer in English. Her work, *The Book of Margery Kempe*, recounts her conversion and visions, along with her spiritual journey, after her healing from insanity, which followed the birth of her first child. She herself was born in 1373, the year of Julian's revelations, the daughter of a prosperous former mayor of Lynn, a city some forty miles west and slightly north of Norwich. Married to

John Kempe, she persuaded him to undertake a vow of chastity which lasted a matter of years. She saw visions and was given to fits of tears and other forms of emotional outpouring, which were less than popular with some of the congregations she encountered. She also made pilgrimages, journeying as far as Rome and Jerusalem. More important to us, she made a pilgrimage to the cathedral at Norwich and used this visit as an opportunity for a meeting with Julian. She recalls this meeting in her autobiography, offering us direct evidence not only of Julian's existence, but of her role as a counselor:

> Then she made her way to Norwich. . . . The creature was charged and commanded in her soul that she should go to a White Friar in the same city of Norwich. . . . And then she was commanded by our Lord to go to an anchoress in the same city who was called Dame Julian. . . . Great was the holy conversation that the anchoress and this creature had through talking of the love of our Lord Jesus Christ for the many days that they were together (Kempe, pp. 77-78).

The *Book of Margery Kempe* remains a remarkable account of life in the later Middle Ages, although Margery's enthusiasm at times may make its devotional intent less easy to grasp in our age of moderation. Unlike Julian, Margery could literally neither read nor write, so that her work was dictated, and her knowledge of devotional literature would have come from having the works read to her. As previously mentioned, Margery knew of both Richard Rolle's and Walter Hilton's works, though she does not seem to have encountered *The Cloud of Unknowing*. Given Margery Kempe's expansive nature, I find it impossible to suppose that she failed to discuss the works of these mystics during her sojourn with Julian at Norwich.

A lesser figure whose work may have been familiar to Julian was one John Lydgate, a poet and translator of devotional works, who spent much of his life attached to the monastery at Bury St. Edmund's, living from about 1370 until about 1450. His works included *The Pilgrimage of the Life Man*, *The Fall of Princes* and *The Life of Our Lady*. Bury St. Edmund's is only thirty miles from Norwich, so that some contact with Julian is likely.

The Cloud of Unknowing, which appeared at about 1400, does not seem to have been influential upon Julian, since her *Revelations* would in both versions have preceded this anonymous and advanced mystical treatise, written specifically for those intending the life of the contemplative. This does not deter from its position as a major contribution to the English mystical writing of the period.

Thus it can be seen that while Julian may have had knowledge of some of the writing both before and during her time, her work must be allowed to stand on its own, having its own distinct style and purpose, displaying characteristics common to much that had been written in her time but retaining a personality and style that were unique to her. We are left having to admit that her literary style was divinely inspired, but expressed in the language spoken in her day, albeit adapted to the more poetic form of expression that literature demanded. Undoubtedly, her work and these other mystical writings all reflect a common spirit of their age, an age of spiritual exploration and challenge, the first stirrings of a movement which was to blossom and culminate in the Reformation two centuries later.

Julian's Biblical Sources

The importance of scripture to Julian cannot be overemphasized. The whole of her *Revelations* is suffused with a profound knowledge of the Bible. As Julian herself expressed the centrality of scripture in her faith:

> Our faith is founded on God's word, and it belongs to our faith that we believe God's word will be preserved in all things (CW, p.233; ET, pp. 424-25).

Indeed, Julian knew her scriptures sufficiently well that she identifies herself with the disciples in one passage:

> And in this time of joy I could have said with St. Paul: Nothing shall separate me from the love of Christ; and in the pain I could have said with St. Peter: Lord, save me, I am perishing (CW, p. 205; ET, p.355).

How, then, did Julian acquire her scriptural knowledge? Here we are faced with a diversity of opinion. Colledge and Walsh maintain that Julian knew the Vulgate in detail before the writing of her *Short Version of the Revelations*. This requires the acceptance of Julian's ability to read Latin as a result of education in this language in her youth or early adulthood. Colledge and Walsh use her proposed facility in Latin to argue further that Julian had been a nun from an early age and did not become enclosed in her anchorhold until late in her life, in her fifty-first year, following the completion of her Long Version. They base

ιjecture on the will of Roger Reed, which indicates Julian's
⌐.. .. the solitary life as having taken place in 1394. I do not
believe that detailed knowledge of the Vulgate in Latin would
have been necessary for Julian to have acquired a comprehensive
grasp of the scriptures, although it seems likely that whoever
taught her did so from such knowledge, and such translation
which Julian received could have been accurate. It is possible to
suggest that she would have received much scriptural instruction
through sermons, homilies, and devotional works. Her reading of
the daily offices, as described in the *Ancrene Riwle*, would alone
have made her familiar with many of the passages of the Bible
which either appear or are paraphrased in her *Revelations*. An
analysis of the biblical references in the *Revelations* indicates her
especial familiarity with the Psalms, the four Gospels, the Pauline
and Johannine epistles, and Second Isaiah. It is my contention
that her devotional life would have led to a detailed memorization
of these particular segments of the scriptures. She would have
recited the complete psalter in regular rotation, and her presence
at daily recitation of the mass could only have embedded the
epistles and Gospel passages deeply into her consciousness. Her
advocacy of the language of the people has already led me to suggest that she may well have possessed a Bible in the English vernacular, but I admit that this is pure conjecture. Later in this work
I will examine my reasons for suspecting that she was never a
nun, but for now, I believe that we must allow Julian the ability to
have a broad and deep knowledge of the scriptures without forc-
ing her into the mold of classical scholar.

Were one to attempt to analyze fully Julian's scriptural references,
one would have sufficient material for an entire separate book. As
will be seen when the contents of the Revelations are considered,
Julian's scriptural references are constant. Familiarity with more
than fifty books of the Bible as we know it today is evident, a record
with which many a modern theologian would be satisfied.

For the purposes of this brief work, there are seven passages
which I believe form an essential base for an understanding of
Julian's theology;

John 14:15–17
Romans 6:1–11
Romans 8:31–39
2 Corinthians 5:17–21
Galatians 2:19b–20
Philippians 2:5–11
Revelation 21:1–4

6

Julian's Life

The available facts of Julian's life are few. Her statement that she was thirty and a half years old when she had her visions on May 8, 1373, allows us to place her birth in 1342, assuming that half year to be literal. If, however, she was speaking of herself as being well into her thirty-first year, it is of course possible that she was born at the beginning of 1343. We do not know where she was born, although there is a theory that she may have been born and brought up in Yorkshire, based on an analysis of the dialect that is evident in her *Revelations*. We do not know when she came to Norwich. The first hard evidence of her existence in Norwich comes in the form of a mention in the will of Roger Reed in March 1393, which is the first mention of her as an anchoress. There is considerable difference of opinion as to the level of her education. Colledge and Walsh would have her trained in Latin, probable only if she had taken orders as a nun at a reasonably early age, proof of which is negligible. It is at least likely that she was the daughter of a wealthy merchant, since she clearly received considerable education, probably at the hands of a private tutor. Yet it is doubtful that she came from the nobility, since her existence is much more likely to have been recorded had that been the case. She may well have had access to the library of the Benedictine Priory, the nunnery at Carrow, or one of the friaries, but obviously this would have been only through a third party and after her arrival in Norwich, whenever that was.

Since the first mention of her as an anchoress coincides with the date which she herself gives us for the completion of the *Longer Version of the Revelations*, 1393, this would find her enclosed and recognized by her written account at the age of fifty-one. So we can infer a long life for Julian by the standards of her times, before we have any certainty of detail. We are therefore forced to conjecture, based on hints that we can acquire from her written work.

I agree with those scholars who claim that Julian was definitively not a nun. Grace Jantzen summarizes her reasons for this opinion on the following bases:

There is no evidence of the *Revelations* having been written in a convent; Julian writes for her fellow Christians, her "even-Christians," as she calls them, not for religious; Julian makes no reference to sisters in an order; Julian makes no reference to the monastic vows of poverty, chastity, and obedience; there is no discussion or even mention of a rule, although many of her expressions reflect a knowledge of the *Ancrene Riwle* (already discussed); there is no hint of her observance of a monastic timetable or set times for prayer, although it is likely that she followed a pattern of devotion similar or identical to that outlined in the *Ancrene Riwle*; there is no discussion of deference to a prioress or other superior. It must be conceded that her bishop suffers the same neglect; in Jantzen's words, the *Revelations* do not "breathe the air of a convent, let alone a Benedictine convent."

Thus, if one is to accept that in all probability Julian was not a nun, what could she have been up to in those first fifty-one years? It is possible that she had joined one of the communities resembling beguinages, already described earlier in this work, but I tend to believe that her decision to become an anchoress was made as an alternative to this style of life rather than as an addition to it. There is one fact that emerges from Norman Tanner's study of the church in Norwich, based on the examination of wills, which I believe has considerable importance in attempting to establish Julian's early life. At no point in the period which he studied, from 1370 until 1532 were any nuns who had been widowed recorded. It was thus, in all probability, impossible for one who had at some time been married to become a nun. As stated earlier, there was only one nunnery in Norwich, at Carrow, and it would appear that this nunnery did not accept widows into their order. Hence, if Julian had been married, her options were limited, but the lay order of anchoress would have been readily available to her. Beyond this, it is my contention that her whole work breathes an understanding of sexuality more likely to have been acquired by one who had experienced a normal married life, at least for a while. Her confidence in defining both the masculine and feminine natures of Christ, while heavily reliant on divine inspiration, suggests a grasp of the human condition, unlikely to have been absorbed in the narrow confines of convent life with its emphasis on celibacy and chastity.

Accepting the theory that she was born in Yorkshire or there-abouts, it could be posited that she moved to Norwich upon her marriage to a wealthy Norwich merchant, a marriage that could well have taken place when she was about eighteen years of age. This would bring us to the year 1360. Norwich encountered two secondary outbreaks of the Black Death, one in 1361-62 and another in 1369. Julian's husband could have succumbed in either of these, but the apparent absence of children in her life leads me to suggest that he could have died in the outbreak of 1361-62, leaving Julian as a young widow of nineteen or twenty. At this point she could have begun to be absorbed in her theo-logical searchings, culminating in her prayer for the three "graces," the recollection of Christ's Passion, a bodily sickness, and the three wounds of contrition, compassion, and a deep longing for God. She would have then had a period of twelve years (or four years if her husband had died in the 1369 out-break) in which to acquire the level of theological sophistication to understand partially the import of her revelations, as she describes them in the Shorter Version, written shortly after the visions of 1373.

I underline the fact that this suppositon is conjecture, but together with my conviction that Julian was not a nun, it offers a plausible account of the "missing years."

What we do know for certain is that Margery Kempe visited Julian in her cell, for she states this in her autobiography, as described above. The dating of Margery Kempe's visit is not, however, certain, though it is likely to have taken place between 1400 and 1415, the later date seeming to have greater support, particularly bearing in mind Margery Kempe's age. She was born only at about 1373 and did not write her *Book of Margery Kempe* until 1436, when she would have been about sixty-three years old. She would have been forty-two in 1415, and her account of her visit to Julian suggests that she had a considerable life experi-ence to discuss at that point, less probable at the age of twenty-seven in 1400.

The other important references to Julian occur in the wills and bequests, researched by Norman Tanner, which I now list in summary and in chronological order. It should be remembered that one shilling was the equivalent of two days' pay for a skilled laborer in this period (Tanner, p. 200).

March 1393

Roger Reed, Rector of St. Michael's, Coslany, Norwich, leaves two shillings to "Julian Anchorite."

May 19, 1404

In Archbishop Arundel's register: Thomas Edmund, chaplain of Aylsham, bequeathes "to Julian an anchoress at St. Julian's Church Norwich 12 pence and 8d. to Sara living with her" (equals "Juliane anachorite apud ecclesiam St. Juliane in Norwico").

November 24, 1415

In Archbishop Chichele's register: John Plumpton, of Conesford at Norwich, bequeathes "40d. to the anker in the church of St. Julian at Conesford at Norwich, 12d. to her maid-servant and 12d. to a former maid, Alice."

1416

In Archbishop Chichele's register, Isabelle Ufford, Countess of Suffolk, leaves 20 shillings to Julian, "recluz" at Norwich.

1423

There is a reference in a bequest by Walter Daniel to an *incluso* at St. Julian's. This is inconclusive, since Julian should have been referred to as an *inclusa*, in the Latin feminine gender, although it is perfectly possible that Julian was still alive at this time, at an age of eighty-one.

August 1429

Richard Baxter, citizen and merchant of Norwich leaves the following bequest: "Item I bequeath to the anchoress in the churchyard of St. Julian's of Conesford in Norwich 3s.4d." This bequest may have been to the anchoress Julian Lampet, who took possession of her cell in 1426. It is not certain whether Julian Lampet inherited Julian of Norwich's cell or whether she had her own, possibly attached to Carrow Nunnery, which, it will be remembered, owned the patronage of St. Julian's Church. If the Baxter bequest was indeed to Julian of Norwich, this would have brought her to the exceedingly ripe age, for the four-teenth century, of eighty-seven.

I favor the probability that the Baxter bequest was to Julian Lampet, that she indeed took over Julian's cell in 1426, and that Julian herself probably died between 1423 and 1425. The latter date would put her death at the age of eighty-three, an advanced age in years, but not improbably so, for nuns and religious are prone to long life expectancies, because of their sensible living habits and the absence of unusual stress. Blomefield, in his *History of Norfolk*, has Julian alive in 1443, which would make her more than one hundred years old, but it seems clear that he was muddling his Julians (Blomefield, Vol. IV, p. 81).

There is no hard evidence for either the date of Julian's death or her place of burial, nor is there any suggestion that her place of burial became a shrine following her decease. We must therefore await further discoveries before we can pin down these events with any accuracy at all. Her memorial is her written work, and it is to this monumental gift that we now turn our attention.

PART II
THE
REVELATIONS
OF JULIAN
OF NORWICH

"The Crucifixion"
14th Century Retable
St. Luke's Chapel
Norwich Cathedral

7

Julian's Vision

In her Short Version of the *Revelations*, Julian gives a detailed account of both her desire to receive her visions and the form she hoped they would take. Her account of the actual event adheres closely to what she states she was praying for; if anything, the experience was more profound than she had anticipated. It is, of course, possible that Julian adjusted her account of her hopes to conform to her actual experience, but her admission that she received so much more than she had prayed for tends to eliminate this suggestion of hindsight. I have chosen to quote her account of the event and her anticipation of it at considerable length, since the dramatic rendering is difficult to improve upon and forms an essential introduction to all that we shall be examining hereafter. The account in the Short Version is much more explicit concerning the physical details of the *Revelations*, and I have chosen to use it for that reason. The opening paragraph is clearly the work of her scribe:

> Here is a vision shown by the goodness of God to a devout woman, and her name is Julian, who is a recluse at Norwich and still alive, A.D. 1413, in which vision are very many words of comfort, greatly moving for all those who desire to be Christ's lovers.

Julian then takes up the story:

> I desired three graces by the gift of God. The first was to have recollection of Christ's Passion. The second was a bodily sickness, and the third was to have, of God's gift, three wounds. As to the first, it came into my mind with devotion; it seemed to me that I had great feeling for the Passion of Christ, but still I desired to have more by the grace of God. I thought that I

wished that I had been at that time with Mary Magdalen and
with the others who were Christ's lovers, so that I might have
seen with my own eyes our Lord's Passion which he suffered
for me, so that I might have suffered with him as others did
who loved him, even though I believed firmly in all Christ's
pains, as Holy Church shows and teaches, and as paintings of
the Crucifixion represent, which are made by God's grace,
according to Holy Church's teaching, to resemble Christ's
Passion, so far as human understanding can attain. But despite
all my true faith I desired a bodily sight, through which I
might have more knowledge of our Lord and savior's bodily
pains, and of the compassion of our Lady and of all his true
lovers who were living at that time and saw his pains, for I
would have been one of them and have suffered with them. I
never desired any other sight of God or revelation, until my
soul would be separated from the body, for I trusted truly that
I would be saved. My intention was, because of that revelation, to have had truer recollection of Christ's Passion. As to
the second grace, there came into my mind with contrition—a
free gift from God which I did not seek—a desire of my will to
have by God's gift a bodily sickness, and I wished it to be so
severe that it might seem mortal, so that I should in that sickness receive all the rites which Holy Church had to give me,
whilst I myself should believe that I was dying, and everyone
who saw me would think the same, for I wanted no comfort
from any human, earthly life. In this sickness I wanted to have
every kind of pain, bodily and spiritual, which I should have
if I were dying, every fear and every assault from devils, and
every other kind of pain except the departure of the spirit, for
I hoped that this would be profitable to me when I should die,
because I desired soon to be with my God.

. . . When I was young I desired to have that sickness when I
was thirty years old. As to the third . . . I conceived a great
desire, and prayed our Lord God that he would grant me in
the course of my life three wounds, that is, the wound of contrition, the wound of compassion and the wound of longing
with my will for God. Just as I asked for the other two condi-
tionally, so I asked for this third without any condition. The
two desires which I mentioned first passed from my mind,
and the third remained there continually.

And when I was thirty and a half years old, God sent me a
bodily sickness in which I lay for three days and three nights;

and on the fourth night I received all the rites of Holy Church, and did not expect to live until day. But after this I suffered on for two days and two nights, and on the third night I often thought that I was on the point of death; and those who were around me also thought this. But in this I was very sorrowful and reluctant to die, not that there was anything on earth that it pleased me to live for, or anything of which I was afraid, for I trusted in God. But it was because I wanted to go on living to love God better and longer, and living so, obtain grace to know and love God more as he is in the bliss of heaven.

. . . So I lasted until day, and by then my body was dead from the middle downwards, it felt to me. Then I was moved to ask to be lifted up and supported, with cloths held to my head, so that my heart might be more free to be at God's will, and so that I could think of him whilst my life would last; and those who were with me sent for the parson, my curate, to be present at my end. He came with a little boy, and brought a cross; and by that time my eyes were fixed, and I could not speak. The parson set the cross before my face and said: Daughter, I have brought you the image of your savior. Look at it and take comfort from it, in reverence of him who died for you and me. It seemed to me that I was well as I was, for my eyes were set upwards towards heaven, where I trusted that I was going; but nevertheless I agreed to fix my eyes on the face of the crucifix if I could, so as to hold out longer until my end came, for it seemed to me that I could hold out longer with my eyes set in front of me rather than upwards. After this my sight began to fail, and it was all dark around me in the room, dark as night, except that there was ordinary light trained upon the image of the cross, I never knew how. Everything around the cross was ugly to me, as if it were occupied by a great crowd of devils.

After that I felt as if the upper part of my body were beginning to die. My hands fell down on either side, and I was so weak that my head lolled to one side. The greatest pain that I felt was my shortness of breath and the ebbing of my life. Then truly I believed that I was at the point of death. And suddenly in that moment all my pain left me, and I was as sound, particularly in the upper part of my body, as ever I was before or have been since. I was astonished by this change, for it seemed to me that it was by God's secret doing and not natural; and even so, in this ease which I felt, I had no more confidence that I should live, nor was the ease complete, for I thought that I would rather have been delivered of this world, because that was what my heart longed for (CW, pp. 125–29; ET, pp. 201–209).

In seeking to understand exactly what had happened to Julian, I believe that we must consider the possibility that she was the subject of what today is described as a "near-death" experience, an event which I have myself encountered and which possesses startling similarities to Julian's description above. Hans Küng, the contemporary German theologian, refers to this phenomenon in his work *Eternal Life?* in which he quotes the research of Raymond A. Moody, author of *Life after Life.* In this book, Küng describes the experiences of dying that Moody had encountered, from some 150 cases studied, in part thus:

At some point [the subject] finds himself approaching some sort of barrier or border, apparently representing the limit between earthly life and the next life. Yet he finds that he must go back to the earth, that the time for his death has not yet come. At this point he resists, for by now he is taken up with his experiences in the afterlife and does not want to return. He is overwhelmed by intense feelings of joy, love and peace. Despite his attitude, though, he sometimes reunites with his physical body and lives (Küng, p. 10).

There is much here that is parallel to Julian's description. Another of Moody's subjects gives us further insight:

Now, I think that the voice that was talking to me actually realized that I wasn't ready to die. You know, it was just kind of testing me more than anything else. Yet, from the moment the light spoke to me, I felt really good—secure and loved. The love which came from it is just unimaginable, indescribable. It was a fun person to be with! And it had a sense of humor, too—definitely! (Küng, p. 11)

Most of these near-death experiences have four common ingredients: first, there is a remarkable sense of lightness, both in terms of visual light and a feeling of complete weightlessness; second, there is a sense in which one is viewing one's own body from without; third, there is a feeling that one is absolutely taken care of by an enveloping love of limitless power; and, finally, there is an undeniable sense of fun or humor about the whole experience. Julian to some degree exhibits all of these characteristics.

The cynic will suggest that all of these experiences are merely the hallucinatory workings of a mind that is attempting to counteract the fear of death. It is, of course, at this point that science and faith come into tension. Can what one has felt or sensed be accepted as fact? Could Julian's entire vision be the ravings of one who had suffered from the hallucinations brought on by an extremely high fever? I believe not, for the authenticity of the theology by which Julian was inspired in this event can be dismissed only on the basis that the entire experience of Christianity is an elaborate hoax. There are times when even the most convinced Christian will question the very ground of his or her faith, but as faith once more returns, with renewed strength, I am bound to my conviction that Julian's experience was directly the action of God through the Holy Spirit. It is on this basis that my study of her *Revelations* proceeds. Hans Küng's work is subtitled *Life After Death as a Medical, Philosophical, and Theological Problem*. I believe that Julian would have suggested that life after death was not a problem, that it was not even a possibility, but rather that it was the one certainty upon which our faith is based, won for us on a cross nearly two thousand years ago. The more we study medicine, philosophy, and theology, the more convinced we become that these disciplines cannot be separated, but are different parts of an unified whole, the work of one Creator-God. The joy and laughter that Julian encountered even in the depths of her intense experience are a reminder that faith is a joyous matter. Why would the Creator have given us a sense of humor, but for our enjoyment?—a suggestion that the institutional church has chosen to ignore all too frequently.

One of the great joys for us is that Julian understood the contents of her visions to be for every Christian. The purpose of writing down her interpretation of the revelations was so that they might be shared by what she describes as her "even-Christians," and sharing is an important part of Julian's theology. She believes neither in a heavy hierarchy of faith nor in any exclusiveness for the true believer. Most of all, Julian wanted us to know of God's love for each one of us. This was the ground of all her optimism, a mood that courses through her entire work. Grace Jantzen summarizes Julian's purpose in her *Julian of Norwich*:

But the anchoress herself had another vocation which stood for the conviction that there was also a spiritual hunger, a need for healing and fulfilment even when the material and social conditions of life are adequate. The unhappiness and brokenness of those who formed the wealthier classes of four-teenth-century society needed care and healing as surely as the poor needed shelter and the hungry needed food. Julian found in the experience of the love of God release from guilt and despair, and the resources for the healing of persons. It is this which makes her so significant not only for the poor but also for the affluent and broken society of our time (Jantzen, p.48).

It is my conviction that the reason Julian's theology has recently acquired so much attention is that it speaks precisely to our time and that many of the pressures which we face are remarkably similar to those that I have already described in my review of the time and place in which Julian lived and wrote.

Julian suggests that the principal message and purpose which God has for us is love, a love that cannot be overcome by the powers of this world.

> What, do you wish to know your Lord's meaning in this thing? Know it well, love was his meaning. Who reveals it to you? Love. What did he reveal to you? Love. Why does he reveal it to you? For love. Remain in this, and you will know more of the same. But you will never know different, without end (CW, p. 342; ET, pp. 732-33).

This message of love was given to us in order that we might thus love and therefore live freely. Julian sees Christ's Passion as the supreme manifestation of God's love for us. We are therefore called to share in that Passion as fully as possible. Our Christian belief has to start, not at the foot of the cross, but rather on the very cross itself. This deepest and highest form of love is not something that God does for us, but is rather precisely what God is. We love God because we are loved by him. Julian cannot sep-arate this love from our thought, our reasoning, and our feelings. She espouses a fully integrated theology, encompassed by divine love. If this love is incapable of being overcome, then we live with an indestructible optimism:

> Our good Lord answered to all the questions and doubts which I could raise, saying most comfortingly: I may make all things well, and I can make all things well, and I shall make all things well, and I will make all things well: and you will see for yourself that every kind of thing will be well (CW, p. 229; ET, p. 417).

Julian did not purvey a naive and otherworldly optimism. She was completely down to earth in her understanding of human nature and behavior. She spends a considerable portion of her time in the *Revelations* in debating the origins and effects of sin, but her belief in God's forgiveness is absolute and, in a passage reminiscent of St. Paul's famous paean to charity or divine love, she sees no limit to the power of that "Charite":

> So charity keeps us in faith and in hope. And faith and hope lead us in charity, and in the end everything will be charity (CW, p. 340; ET, p. 727).

Her theology has a distinctly Pauline flavor, and it is nowhere stronger than in her belief that "love was God's meaning." It is toward the detailed examination of this "lesson in love" that we now turn.

8

The Contents of Julian's Visions

Julian envisioned three categories of the divine love which has just been described: uncreated charity, created charity and charity given. In brief, uncreated charity is the love within God, experienced within the Trinity; created charity is the love of the Trinity for mankind and therefore defines our soul in God; charity given is our human response in the love of God and defines our purpose in life.

The *Revelations* are divided into chapters which do not form a logical division of the contents. What follows is a summary of the contents, based on the extensive work of Brant Pelphrey. I have added subject headings as a broad guide to the matter included in the relevant section, which on several occasions contains more than one chapter. Some editions have summaries at the beginning of each chapter. These are not particularly helpful later additions and I have ignored them with the intention of preventing further confusion.

Chapters 1–3: Julian Introduces Her Visions

Introduction, including a description of the events that accompanied Julian's experience of the visions, described above from her account in the Short Version.

Chapter 4: A Vision of Christ: Christ Within the Trinity

A vision of the head of Christ, crowned with thorns, beginning to bleed. Julian feels herself as being touched directly by the Trinity. As Pelphrey describes it:

The Trinity is to be understood whenever we see Jesus, because Jesus is God, and God, the Trinity. And God makes

known to us that he is our Maker, our Keeper, and our everlasting Lover (Pelphrey, p.93).

God wills that we should know him. The marvel of the incarnation is that God comes down to us in fully human form so that
we might be able to gain an understanding of who God is in our
own terms.

Chapter 5: God in Creation

God is seen as our Maker, our Keeper, and our Lover. Next to
God, all creation is to be compared to a hazelnut in God's hand,
tiny and insignificant, but of infinite worth to God. Because God
wants us to know him, he gives us a yearning for him, which is
the Holy Spirit at work in us.

Chapter 6: Prayer Direct to God

As God wants us to be in relationship to him, it is better for us
to pray directly to God and not through other means, such as a
saint or a relic. There is nothing too lowly or insignificant to be
loved by God, even our most earthy bodily functions, which
Julian illustrates without restraint.

Chapters 7–10: A Homely, Close God

God is "meek" and "homely," not distant and fiercesome. We
are loved by Jesus and we love him, thus we are bound to all
people and all things, sharing God's love for them, not as a result
of a demand upon us, but through the very sharing of God's love.

Chapter 10: God Shown Among Us

God's will for us is that we should know him as he really is. In
order to achieve this, God has shown himself to us in human
form, suffering the pain of sin himself.

Chapters 11–14: The Challenge of Evil

What does it mean to trust God completely? Faith is understanding that God does all things and that therefore all things, in
whatever form they appear to us, are done well. In an abiding
sense, there is no wrath in God, who is perfect love. What then is
evil and why does it exist? We can be certain that God does not

sin, as Christ was human, yet without sin, and, because of the cross, evil and sin have been overcome and have no power over us, in the long run. We will certainly be rewarded according to our deeds, but in the positive sense that the slightest service in God's love by us merits God's highest gratitude. It is indeed possible that God can be angry at the sin which we commit while retaining his perfect love for us, the sinners. This would account for Julian's statement that God views us "with pity, not with blame."

Chapter 15: The Role of Suffering

Sometimes we suffer, which is the consequence of sin. But suffering is not punishment for our sins; it serves to remind us of our need for God.

Chapters 16–26: Compassion and the Cross

As Pelphrey describes this section:

The compassion which Jesus felt, and feels, for us becomes our own compassion for all humanity. We see the world only in light of the cross, but as though from the cross. There is no way to apprehend God except in this experience of union in the crucified Christ; he is our only revelation of God, and in him—on the cross—we find heaven (Pelphrey, p.95).

This summary, for me, captures the core of Julian's resurrection theology and, as I have already stated, provides us with the ultimate example of the love which God has shown to us and which we are called to give to God in return.

Chapters 27–28: The Nature of Sin

Sin is not something that God does. It is not anything that is done. Sin is, rather, a relationship or the lack of a relationship, not an activity. The pain that results from sin is very real to us and can be seen, whereas sin itself cannot be seen. Yet this pain has the positive effect of warning us of the danger in which we have placed our relationship to God.

Sin requires compassion, not judgment. We do not need to judge anyone, but ought rather to see others with compassion, in the same way that God sees us, with pity and not with blame.

Chapters 29–34: Two Kinds of Truth

The first form of truth is the truth of salvation, which is made known to us, through Christ.

The second form of truth is God's secret truth, which we will not know in this life, but which will explain all the apparent paradoxes and inconsistencies, many of which surround our failure to grasp the necessity of sin and evil in a world that God has made.

Chapters 35–36: Good and Evil Leading to Reconciliation

We have seen that God does all things, and does them well. Everything "bad" or "good" is working toward our reconciliation to God. For example, good often flows from our response to tragedy, sickness, and the death of another.

Chapters 37–46: God's Judgment: The Absence of Wrath and the Lack of Need for Forgiveness

Though we continue to sin, we have already been saved. Can the Christian therefore expect to be perfected in this life? In a word: No. God shows that we will continue to sin until we are taken from this life, yet every soul that is to be "saved" has been saved by God from the beginning, an illustration of the "timelessness" of God. God judges us according to what God intended us to be, which is the extent to which we have taken on the model of Christ Jesus, the perfect human. In this life we will never assume our true nature, our true "self," apart from our recognizing that nature in Christ. We can thus become aware of our true selves only in faith.

There is neither wrath nor forgiveness from God's point of view, because nothing has changed in God's love for us, which is in no way modified by the sins we commit. We should, however, remain aware of the risk of antinomianism, that heresy which proclaims that if we are always forgiven by God, the more we sin, the greater will be the forgiveness we receive from God. St. Paul is as clear on this in the sixth chapter of his epistle to the Romans, referred to earlier, as is Julian throughout her writing.

Perhaps the best way to understand this theology of the lack of need for forgiveness is to accept that God does not need to forgive us, since he has already done so, but we continue to need to feel forgiven.

Chapters 50–52: *The Lord and the Servant: A Parable of Sin and Redemption*

Why do we go on sinning? Julian answers this question with the parable of the Lord and the Servant. In this parable, Julian sees a great lord, clothed in the sky and seated on a throne. The throne is in a desert, and a ragged servant stands before it. The servant turns to perform an errand and falls into a chasm from which he is unable to rise. The lord lifts the servant from the chasm, and the peasant is immediately transfigured: he is clothed in a shining robe and stands at the right hand of the lord.

When we fall, or sin, Christ is present to heal us: the servant is lifted out of the ditch and glorified.

At another level, Christ is himself also the servant, the Suffering Servant of Second Isaiah, who identifies himself with the fallen Adam, the Passover Victim whose sacrifice leads to our salvation, "For as in Adam all [men] die, even so in Christ shall all be made alive" (*Book of Common Prayer*, p. 46).

For God, our salvation occurs at the same time (or "non-time") as our own creation, because of the "timelessness of God." There cannot therefore be any "presalvation" history for God, and this eliminates any sense of predestination for man. There are, however, moments when Julian's view shows tendencies to limit God's salvation to those who believe, thus avoiding any inclination toward universalism.

Chapters 54–57: *Christ in Us, the Cause for Rejoicing*

We are therefore bound to rejoice, on the basis of our union to God, which has already been established for us in Christ. Christ already dwells in us, and to experience the Christian life is to experience the ultimate joy of Christ working within each one of us, individually.

Chapters 58–62: *Jesus, the Church*

Jesus is much more than a remote "savior," and is really present to us at all times as Father, Mother, and intimate Lover. As individuals, we will experience our own brokenness and pain, but the church as a body will not be allowed to be broken apart. The purpose of the church is to surround us, its members, with the love of Jesus. We cannot thus live the life of Christ aside from the church, for Christ is the church.

Chapters 63–72: Our Abhorrence of Sin

In understanding God's absolute love for us, we can begin to hate sin for what it does to our human nature, for it is a perversion of our true nature and alienates us from our intended right relationship to God. We can only abhor a force that has this effect on our earthly existence and denies us the foretaste of heaven that God intends for us.

Chapters 74–77: Different Fears, Both Good and Bad

Some kinds of fear or dread are to be welcomed, for they help us in our process of being restored and reconciled to God. Naked fear has a purging effect upon us. Dread helps us to realize our need for God. Even a near-death experience helps this. Despair makes us long for God. Reverent dread leads us to respect for God and springs from our love for God. It is impossible for love and dread to exist without each other, as might be seen in the love-fear relationship between a child and a parent. There is, however, nothing to be gained from our dwelling on or wallowing in our own sinfulness, because we will never be able to appreciate fully the evil nature of sin and how completely displeasing it is to God, an understanding which, if acquired, would lead us to the depths of despair.

Chapters 78–86: Looking Ahead to God in Jesus, Not Backward at Our Sins

We are reassured that although we will sin, this is only part of a life which will eventually be made sinless and perfect when we achieve our full presence with God in the next life. This process of salvation is constantly at work in us already. We ought therefore to look to Jesus, the source of our true life, rather than spend too much time looking at ourselves. Concentrating on self may lead to a glorying in our imperfections, which borders on pride. Christ has given himself to us in the church, along with our various, individual gifts. As Pelphrey concludes this section: "The greatest gift that we can offer in return, and the only way in which we can truly please God, is to understand his love for us and to rejoice in that love" (Pelphrey, p.101).

PART III
JULIAN'S THEOLOGY

English School, Fourteenth Century, Ivory Corpus
(From the Victoria and Albert Museum, London,
by Courtesy of the Board of Trustees)

9

Trinitarian and Christocentric

First of all, it must be said that Julian's theology was a revealed theology and not the result of a scholastic exercise. Therefore, it is not simple to render it in a systematic treatment. It is necessary to extract it from the *Revelations*, whose attraction in part springs from the repetition of the principal themes throughout the work. In this chapter, I will be giving the broad outline of Julian's theology, in order to establish the general principles. I will then treat the main areas of her theological concern in greater depth in subsequent chapters. It is impossible to attach Julian to any one school of theology, and while it is apparent that she would have been influenced by many who had come before her, her theology is essentially individualized and independent. As Edmund Colledge has said:

> "Part of Julian's greatness is her exceptional independence of . . . external influence, that her Revelations are a singularly pure distillation of her own experiences of mystical rapture, sanctified by long years of prayerful meditation" (Colledge, p. 83).

Julian's theology is both strongly Trinitarian and fundamentally Christocentric. For her, the Trinitarian nature of the Godhead is such that the threefold nature of this Godhead is reflected throughout her theology. It is therefore no coincidence that so much of her definition of her theology comes to us in threefold groupings. In reviewing the contents of the *Revelations*, I have already referred to Julian's three aspects of divine love: uncreated charity, created charity and charity given, describing uncreated charity as the love within God, created charity as the love of the Trinity for mankind, and charity given as the human response to and in the love of God. These three elements reflect three principal theological interests for Julian, respectively: the nature of the being of God; the incarnation and atonement (or, how God reaches humanity in Christ); and humanity's response to God. The Trinity is the strongly combining factor that unites all the attributes of divine love:

> For the Trinity is God, God is the Trinity, the Trinity is our maker, the Trinity is our protector, the Trinity is our everlast-ing lover, the Trinity is our endless joy and our bliss, by our Lord Jesus Christ and in our Lord Jesus Christ. And this was revealed in the first vision and in them all, for where Jesus appears the blessed Trinity is understood, as I see it (CW, p.181; ET, pp. 295–96).

This passage underlines Julian's Trinitarian thinking, at the same time emphasizing the Christocentric nature of her theology. For Julian, the incarnate Jesus is true God, and God the Father cannot be approached independently of Christ, who came to us in order to reveal the Trinity to us in the fullness of its self-giving love. This was not a new understanding. The Trinity is revealed to humanity through Christ, and whatever Julian knew about God, she received through her knowledge of and identification with the crucified Christ. It is through Christ that we are "oned" to God. Our union with God takes place in the very person of Jesus Christ who is himself both God and man. It is through the person of Christ that the uncreated Trinity enters creation to form a spiritual union with humanity. Christ is the essential link, therefore, between God and humanity. The church is the way in which Christ continues to provide that link, and the church, in this sense is Christ, as Julian describes it:

> And therefore it is a certain thing, and good and gracious to will, meekly and fervently, to be fastened and united to our mother Holy Church, who is Christ Jesus (CW, pp. 301–302; ET, pp. 607–608).

For Julian, the church is Christ, because he is in the church; he created it as an act of his love, and we are received by Christ when we turn to the church. She never wavers in her mainte-nance of the fact that transformation of the soul can take place only within the church. When we receive Christ by turning to the church, we are receiving God, in that, for God, there is no distinction to be made between Christ and the church since they are inseparable:

> He is the foundation, he is the substance, he is the teacher, he

is the end, he is the reward for which every loving soul labors (CW, p. 236; ET, p.431).

When we turn to Christ, as the church, he feeds us, as a mother feeds her children, in the eucharist:

> The mother can give her child to suck of her milk, but our precious Mother Jesus can feed us with himself, and does, most courteously and most tenderly, with the blessed sacrament, which is the precious food of true life (CW, p. 298; ET, p. 596).

The threefold definition of her theology moves far beyond Julian's adherence to the Trinitarian formulation. We have already seen that prior to her visions, she had prayed for three gifts of grace: an understanding of the Passion of Christ, the experience of a physical sickness, and a realization of three wounds. These wounds were true contrition, loving compassion, and a longing for the will of God. Julian extended her threefold identifications yet further, describing three kinds of knowledge, three actions, three properties, and three degrees of bliss in heaven.

The three kinds of knowledge or "knowings" that the Christian was to seek were to know God, to know oneself, and to know oneself as being opposed to sin. This knowledge will begin the process of transforming us from the life of sin and our "oneing" to God, as Julian expressed it:

> We ought to have three kinds of knowledge. The first is that we know our Lord God. The second is that we know ourselves, what we are through him in nature and in grace. The third is that we know humbly that our self is opposed to our sin and our weakness (CW, p. 321; ET, p. 665).

The three actions have to do with our relationship to God. We are to seek God; we are to abide in God's love; and we are to trust in God.

Our adherence to these three actions will allow us to experience more fully the three "properties" of God—life, light, and love, of which Julian, along with St. Paul, believes love to be the greatest of the three.

Our threefold benefits are not limited to this life, for, on attaining the heavenly kingdom, we will experience three degrees of bliss: We will receive worship and thanks; we will see this worship and thanks being shared by all; and this worship and thanks will be endless.

Breaking away from this threefold pattern, Julian sees humanity as possessing a dual nature, perhaps in reflection of the human and divine natures of Christ. Humanity, for Julian, has two natures, the sensual and the substantial. It is important to recognize that these two natures do not conform to what we might expect, given the current meaning of these two words. For Julian, our substance is our being itself, whose true expression is to be found in our souls. Our sensuality is all the individual traits that we acquire in our worldly existence, experienced through our senses. We are made sensual when life is breathed into us. All three persons of the Trinity share our substance, which will remain forever joined to that Trinity or Godhead. Only the Son, who became incarnate, shares our sensuality. Thus, our sensual self is our earthly, empirical self, while our substance is our spiritual selfhood. It is our sensuality that is subject to falling into disrepair, through sin. God preserves our substance intact. The task of the Christian is to reunite the senses with the substance, and this is the purpose of our spiritual endeavors.

In our spiritual life, we are to attempt to imitate Christ, who gave us a model of one who had united his substance with his sensuality perfectly. As we find the Christ in us, we will be achieving the reunification of our own substance with our sensuality, and will thus be "oned" once more to God. To achieve this we must die with Christ so that we may share in his resurrection, which Julian tells us is possible only through our total sharing in Christ's Passion. As St. Paul stated it in his epistle to the Galatians:

> I have been crucified with Christ; it is no longer I who live, but Christ who lives in me, and the life I now live in the flesh I live by faith in the Son of God, who loved me and gave himself for me (Galatians 2:20).

For Julian, faith begins on the cross. However, the identification of the individual with the crucified Christ is not sufficient. As I have already suggested, faith, for Julian, can be lived out only within the church, and our spiritual endeavors can be effective only if they are made within the context of the community of faith. Her isolation as an anchoress must have left Julian particularly aware of the need to remain identified with the Christian community at large, in spite of a discipline which kept her in that isolation. Throughout her work, Julian not only emphasizes that her *Revelations* were for all her "even-Christians," but she is clear on the need for sharing and participation in the life of faith, a sharing modeled for us by Christ himself during his ministry among us. In fact, for Julian, the work has already been done for us, by Christ, who has brought us to life. Our task is to acknowledge the new life which is thus within us and to be "oned" to that which is ours through the work of the Creator-God, to whom our attention must now be turned.

God as Creator

As the reader may have by now come to expect, Julian sees God as our Creator in a threefold role, as Maker, Keeper, and Lover. That God should perform these functions for us is the ground of our optimism. Such is the power of God the Creator, that in attempting to understand it we should liken the world to a hazelnut, as Julian describes it:

> And in this he showed me something small, no bigger than a hazelnut, lying in the palm of my hand, as it seemed to me, and it was as round as a ball. I looked at it with the eyes of my understanding and thought: What can this be? I was amazed that it could last, for I thought that because of its littleness it would suddenly have fallen into nothing. And I was answered in my understanding: It lasts and always will, because God loves it; and thus everything has being through the love of God.
>
> In this little thing I saw three properties. The first is that God made it, the second is that God loves it, the third is that God preserves it (CW, p.183; ET, pp. 299–300).

With this passage, Julian encourages us to recognize that nothing in creation is too small for God's love, with its infinite power and infinite concern.

A doctrine of creation is an essential prerequisite to a doctrine of salvation, and Julian links the two acts of God in her theological understanding, since they both spring from God's unswerving love for us:

> . . . that he who created it [i.e. all things] created everything for love, and by the same love it is preserved (CW, p. 190; ET, p. 318).

This love springs from the goodness of God and of everything that God has created:

> For God is everything which is good, as I see, and the good-
> ness which everything has is God. . . . For God is everything
> that is good, as I see; and God has made everything that is
> made, and God loves everything that he has made. . . . For
> God is in man and God is all (CW, pp. 191–92; ET, p. 322).

From these quotations, two emphases emerge which are important aspects of Julian's theology of creation. First is the understanding of God's immanence and second is God's infinite goodness. Both of these qualities are within God's essential nature:

> God is essence in his very nature; that is to say, that goodness
> which is natural is God. He is the ground, he is the substance,
> he is the very essence or nature, and he is the true Father and
> the true Mother of natures. And all natures which he has
> made to flow out of him to work his will, they will be restored
> and brought back into him by the salvation of man, through
> the operation of grace (CW, pp. 302–303; ET, pp. 611–12).

Here Julian herself makes the link between creation and salvation, which St. Paul alludes to in the eighth chapter of his epistle to the Romans:

> For the creation waits with eager longing for the revealing of
> the children of God (Romans 8:19).

This thought of Julian's bears remarkable affinity with the thinking of St. Francis, as exemplified in his *Hymn to the Sun*. It also bears a strong resemblance to the creational theology of Thomas Aquinas, with whose systematic theology Julian is not always in agreement.

It is also the work of this same Creator-God to bestow upon us our brother and savior, the incarnate Christ, to give us that part of himself and, in so doing, to demonstrate that the motivation for our creation was love and love alone, not domination or subjection:

> So it is with our Lord Jesus and us, for truly it is the greatest
> possible joy, as I see it, that he who is highest and mightiest,
> noblest and most honorable, is lowest and humblest, most
> familiar and courteous. . . . For the greatest abundance of joy
> which we shall have, as I see it, is this wonderful courtesy and
> familiarity of our Father, who is our Creator, in our Lord Jesus
> Christ, who is our brother and our savior (CW, pp. 188–89;
> ET, pp. 314–15).

The cross, for Julian, is the Creator's ultimate act of self-giving love, proof of God's all-goodness. How then, can a Creator who is all good, allow evil to exist? How can such a God countenance such tragedies as the Black Death in the fourteenth century or AIDS in the current day?

For Julian the answer is twofold. First, evil exists because of God's choice of self-limitation, a choice made by God in order to allow humanity its freedom of choice in its actions here on earth. Second, it is not given to us to understand evil, but we are constantly assured by God that all shall be well, and that what appears to be evil and the opposite of well to us, may not have the same characteristics in God's eyes. We still have difficulty in explaining essential evil, as, for instance, in the Holocaust, and we can say that good arises even from such evil, but how can this be the work of a merciful, loving God? Julian struggles with this challenge throughout her *Revelations*, and the subject will occupy us more fully when we examine Julian's theology of sin. For now we must, with Julian, accept the necessity of sin in God's economy, for:

> Sin is necessary, but all will be well, and all will be well, and every kind of thing will be well (CW, p. 225; ET, p. 405).

Julian encourages us to recognize that for God, the impossible becomes possible:

> And to this I had no other answer as a revelation from our Lord except this: What is impossible to you is not impossible to me. I shall preserve my word in everything, and I shall make everything well (CW, p. 233; ET, p. 426).

We are left, with Julian, having to trust God in a matter which remains concealed to us in this life, but which, we are assured, will be revealed to us when we are fully "oned" to God in the next life. For this life, we must be content to realize the dwelling of a merciful God within us, and to accept that presence with thankful joy:

> Greatly ought we to rejoice that God dwells in our soul; and more greatly ought we to rejoice that our soul dwells in God. Our soul is created to be God's dwelling place, and the dwelling of our soul is God, who is uncreated. It is a great understanding to see and know inwardly that God, who is our Creator, dwells in our soul, and it is a far greater understand-

ing to see and know inwardly that our soul, which is created, dwells in God in substance, of which substance, through God, we are what we are (CW, p. 285; ET, pp. 561-62).

Our identity is thus a fact of our creation. Whoever we are, whatever we do, however we appear to ourselves, we are worthwhile to God, who created us out of love in order to love us, whether we recognize this fact or not. God has given us the independence to fail to make this recognition, but our independence, great though it may appear to be, is not absolute. We did not, for instance, choose to be born. But we do have, within boundaries, freedom of thought and behavior, which results in our individuality. Thus while we share God's "substance," we also possess a distinct character aside from God.

In spite of our propensity for making the wrong choices, for opting to be and act in an un-Godlike manner, God, according to Julian, still sees humanity as the crowning glory of his creation:

> For it is revealed that we are his crown, which crown is the Father's joy, the Son's honor, the Holy Spirit's delight, and endless marvellous bliss to all who are in heaven (CW, p. 278; ET, p. 544).

Borrowing the allegory of Julian's parable of the Lord and the Servant, the servant ceases to be the wretched, naked, and pitiable creature and joins the lord in splendid joy. Our task, as servants, is to begin the process of becoming who God the Creator intends us to be, by realizing our very fullest potential, which can be achieved only in full partnership with God. Julian expresses this in a prayer that I find tremendously useful in centering myself on God:

> God, of your goodness give me yourself, for you are enough for me, and I can ask for nothing which is less which can pay you full worship. And if I ask for anything which is less, always I am in want; but only in you do I have everything (CW, p. 184; ET, p. 302).

Divine love has three principal tasks: the act of creation of humanity, which includes our capacity for God; the act of the maturing or increasing of humanity, in which we are remade in Christ; and the act of our perfecting or fulfilling through the indwelling Christ. In these acts, the Creator wills the first, the Son effects the second, and the Holy Spirit inspires the third. Julian, correctly, does not divorce the action of the Creator from the unity of the Trinity, but sees different roles for the various persons of the Trinity in the fulfillment of the Creator's intention, an intention suffused by joy:

> Therefore God rejoices in the creature and the creature in God, endlessly marvelling, in which marvelling he sees God, his Lord, his Maker, so exalted, so great and so good in comparison with him who is made that the creature scarcely seems anything to itself. But the brightness and clearness of truth and wisdom makes him see and know that he is made for love (CW, p. 256; ET, pp. 484–85).

This love which our Creator-God shows to us is most profoundly made manifest to us in the incarnation, life, ministry, and Passion of his Son.

Christ as Keeper, Mediator, and Mother: Julian's Christology

As I have already suggested, Julian's Christology lies at the very heart of her theology, and at the center of this Christology stands her emphasis on our need for identification with the crucified Christ. This is for her where faith begins for humanity, where God made his ultimate gift for us out of his uncompromising love for the human race. Two texts, already referred to, are seminal to Julian's thinking: "I have been crucified with Christ; and it is no longer I who live, but it is Christ who lives in me" (Galatians 2:19); and "Let the same mind be in you that was in Christ Jesus, who . . . emptied himself, taking the form of a slave . . . and became obedient to the point of death—even death on a cross" (Philippians 2:5-8).

Julian's desire to share in the Passion of Christ, which she described as one of the experiences she earnestly prayed for prior to her visions, was not inconsistent with the theological direction of her times. However, she took it to a new and personal level, perhaps most reminiscent of St. Francis and his desire for the physical manifestation of the stigmata. Like St. Paul, Julian was not content to understand the Passion, but sought full physical sharing in it. Compassion, one of the "three wounds" that Julian sought, which means in Latin "to share with," for Julian involved total sharing with the crucified Christ as a model for the compassion we are called to show to all as Christians. For Julian the need to be so absolutely identified with Christ has to do with her sense of the purpose of our existence, which, in reflection of the dual nature of Christ, is to be transformed from our human nature to our divine nature through our identification with Christ, whom God sent that we might fullfill the purpose for which God the Creator made us.

Thus Julian's life, her vocation as an anchoress, and the writing down of her revelations are all consistent with her desire to experience the indwelling Christ and to share that experience with her "even-Christians." Julian expounds the orthodox Christian belief that Christ dwells continuously in our souls, whether we are aware of this fact or not. She refers to this indwelling as follows:

> The place which Jesus takes in our soul he will nevermore vacate, for in us is his home of homes and his everlasting dwelling (CW, p. 313; ET, p.641).

If humanity wishes to understand itself, this is not to be achieved by looking at ourselves, a particularly popular occupation in current times, but rather by looking into the person of Jesus Christ. We share in Christ's humanity in order to share in his divinity, most particularly in our own resurrection. The love that God showed for us in Christ had no beginning, but is and was part of God's timeless purpose. When God looks at humanity, God sees the life of Christ, whom he sent to be our Mediator; and when God judges humanity, he does so only in the light of Christ's offering of himself to atone for our sins, and this explains why our salvation has already been assured, in spite of the evil in which we become enmeshed.

We thus see ourselves most fully when we look at Christ, for he shows us our fullest potential. We see in Christ what God intends us to be, what we can become by God's grace and the process by which we can realize our potential, which has already begun through the working of the Son and the Holy Spirit. By looking at Christ we can also see what we are not, where we have failed, and thus we are made more aware of the nature of our sin, the first step toward our transformation, the admission of what needs to be changed. But this, for Julian, is not the ground for despair or self-reproach, but the source of optimism and joy, because we recognize that, good or bad, we are "ever in Christ's loving" and that, in the familiar words of St. Paul, "nothing can separate us from the love of God, which is in Christ Jesus" (Romans 8:39).

God and humanity meet in Christ. Goodness and the immanence of God are realized in human creation. And yet evil persists in manifesting itself in the world. This puzzles Julian, who is occupied throughout her *Revelations* with a struggle to explain the existence of sin, a matter that will be dealt with in its own chapter. She finally resolves the issue in her parable of the Lord and the Servant and her explanation of God's great secret deed, which will make all things well in the end, when God chooses. In spite of this problem of the human propensity for evil, Julian maintains that humanity remains God's best creative effort. She sees creation as God's eternal intention, and whatever the difficulties with sin and evil, Julian understands that we are of infinite value and worth to God, as indicated by the love shown to us by the Passion of Christ. This infinite worth is extended to all of God's human creatures; hence our need to take seriously our baptismal promise to "respect the dignity of every human being" (*Book of Common Prayer*, p. 305).

God's ultimate purpose is that we should truly know him and be totally united to him. To achieve this knowledge and to effect this relationship, God sent to earth himself in the form of his only Son. The union or "oneing" of God and humanity takes place specifically in the person of Christ, who is both man and God, expressed by Julian as follows:

> For we know in our faith, and it was also revealed in all this, that Christ Jesus is both God and man; and in his divinity he is himself supreme bliss, and was from without beginning, and he will be without end, which true everlasting bliss cannot of its nature be increased or diminished. And this was plentifully seen in every revelation, and especially in the twelfth, where he says: I am he who is highest. And with respect to Christ's humanity, it is known in our faith and it was also revealed that with all the power of his divinity, for love, to bring us to his bliss, he suffered pains and Passion and died. And these are the deeds of Christ's humanity, in which he rejoices (CW, p.230; ET, p.418–19).

It is Christ's total humanity that assures us of our eventual total divinity, and we are bound to God in three distinct ways. We have the human capacity to be at one with God, since, out of God's love for us he created us in his own image, thus sharing in his nature, which Julian refers to as our "substantial" selves. Second, we experience our dwelling in God through our being at one with Christ. Third, the Holy Spirit is continuously active in "oneing" us into the experiential reality of our selves united with God. We as humans find this fulfillment by participating in God's "charity," by loving, and by being loved. For we have an infinite capacity to love God, often sadly unrealized. We have, indeed, three powers that contribute to our "likeness" to God: we can do the things we want to do; we can know things; and we have the capacity to love, in the fullest sense of that word. These three powers—doing, knowing, and loving—reflect the activities of the Trinity, of Father, Son, and Holy Spirit, or Creator, Wisdom, and Love. This will be examined further when the theology of "oneing" is discussed later in this work.

Julian's Christocentrism has already been stated, but needs to be emphasized beside her strong identification with the Trinity. I have suggested that Julian has much in common with the Franciscan way of thinking theologically. This commonality is displayed in four major ways. Julian shares the Franciscan concept of the Trinity's relationship to time, in which God exists outside time, yet nevertheless pervades space and time. Julian shares the Franciscan concern for all of nature as "all that God loves." She expresses a strongly Franciscan desire for union with Christ and she accepts the concept of God's universal love for all human beings, thus questioning our temporal view of divine judgment. Having thus branded Julian as a Franciscan, it is necessary to point out that she "borrowed" her theology from many separate traditions. We should remember too that in Norwich she had easy access through the priory and the friaries to a wide variety of traditions. Therefore, we can either therefore state that Julian was an Augustinian-Dominican-Benedictine-Franciscan-Carmelite, familiar with Anselmic ideas, or we can content ourselves by recognizing that her theology was highly individualistic, and not subject to convenient theological "pigeonholing." For all that, it remains profoundly Trinitarian, strongly Christocentric, and remarkably orthodox. As Pelphrey summarizes Julian's Christology:

> Julian recognizes that our relationship to the life of Christ is far more than simply our ability to learn about it. For her, our lives are bound up with his life. Whatever is true of him, can be true of us, and by God's grace is in fact true of us already. Christ lives in our own souls, and to know ourselves, we must know him. This fact is at the heart of the *Revelations*, one of its most important insights (Pelphrey, p. 175).

Julian says the same thing, in her inimitable way:

> And this was said in the sixteenth revelation, where it says: The place that Jesus takes in our soul he will never depart

from. And all the gifts which God can give to the creature he has given to his Son Jesus for us, which gifts he, dwelling in us, has enclosed in him until the time that we are fully grown, our soul together with our body and our body together with our soul. Let either of them take help from the other, until we have grown to full stature as creative nature brings about; and then in the foundation of creative nature with the operation of mercy, the Holy Spirit by grace breathes into us gifts leading to endless life (CW, p.287; ET, p. 567).

Christ, then, as mediator, is for Julian our way to God and our means of knowing God. For Julian, in an age much given to praying to God through the mediation of the saints, the veneration of relics and the multiple means provided for paying one's way to God, Christ was the sole mediator, although in keeping with her times, Julian held special reverence for the Virgin Mary, mother of Christ. Her insistence on Christ's effectiveness as sole mediator relied upon the purity of faith found in the earliest church:

> I believe and understand the ministration of holy angels, as scholars tell, but it was not revealed to me; for God himself is nearest and meekest, highest and lowest, and he does everything, and not only all that we need, but also he does everything which is honourable for our joy in heaven; and when I say that he waits for us, moaning and mourning, that means all the true feelings which we have in ourselves, in contrition and in compassion, and all the moaning and mourning because we are not united with our Lord. And as such is profitable, it is Christ in us; and though some of us feel it seldom, it never leaves Christ until the time when he has brought us out of all our woe (CW, p. 336; ET, pp. 710–11).

Never is Christ's role as Mediator more evident than in Julian's interpretation of Christ as our Mother. This is a highly developed part of her theology for which she has become noted in recent times, and deservedly so, for it forms one of Julian's most original and most profound contributions to our theological understanding. The concept of Christ as our Mother was not original to Julian. It is a biblical concept, occurring in Matthew 23:37. St. Paul, hardly the favorite of most feminist theologians, spoke of a world in which there would be "no longer Jew or Greek, there is no longer slave or free, there is no longer male and female; for all of you are one in Christ Jesus" (Galatians 3:28). But Julian goes far beyond a vision of equality between sexes and urges us to understand that Christ possessed the characteristics of the feminine so fully that he can be considered the model for all motherhood. She thus takes an existing concept and expresses it with a fresh urgency and a greater emphasis than had been encountered before her time and which it has taken the church six centuries to rediscover, let alone absorb. The concept came to Julian in her visions, but it was not until the completion of the Long Version of the *Revelations* that she expressed it fully, having spent twenty years meditating on the meaning of this particular facet of her understanding of Christ's nature.

It is in his role as nurturing Mother that Christ becomes most truly representative of the church as God intended it to be. Indeed, for Julian, as the church is our Mother and Christ is the church, so Christ is our Mother:

> And therefore it is a certain thing, and good and gracious to will, meekly and fervently, to be fastened and united to our mother Holy Church, who is Christ Jesus (CW, pp. 301–302; ET, pp. 607–608).

Christ reflects the role of mother, both in his sharing of the task of creation and as one who is prepared to make the ultimate sacrifice of a mother for the child she has nurtured. He is in these ways the model of perfect motherhood, providing the bond between our humanity and his own humanity, comparable to a mother-child relationship. Christ's love for us shares the characteristics of maternal love in combining love with authority and power over his children. In his ministry, Passion, and his sacrificial giving of himself for us, he demonstrates his motherly desire to heal our illnesses and his maternal willingness to suffer in our place, as a mother will wish to take the place of her sick or hurting child.

As with our own parents, Christ remains our Mother even when we have "grown up" spiritually. We begin to realize, of course, that the process of growing up spiritually is never complete in this life, and we never cease to need Christ our Mother as a mother. Motherhood, which may be initiated by the single action of birth, ceases at that point to be a single event or vision and becomes a relationship that cannot be terminated or severed, whatever the child does or desires:

> And our savior is our true Mother, in whom we are endlessly born and out of whom we shall never come (CW, p.292; ET, p.580).

The motherhood we experience in this life has much to teach us about the nature of God's love for us, because it reflects God's love for us, since it is divinely created and inspired. The Passion is the ultimate example of a mother's suffering love, as has already been suggested, proof to us that we have a Mother who will do absolutely anything for us. Therefore, we are as his children able to trust our Mother Christ implicitly—the basis of love between any parent and child—knowing that, as children, we shall sin, again and again, in spite of statements that we are sorry and do not intend to sin again. We know that we shall be disciplined and even find relief in having accepted the rewards for our misbehavior. We also know that we shall be brought up in Christ's love and that love is the motivation behind everything Christ has done, does, and will do for us. All this knowledge makes our progress as God's children possible and bearable, through all the ups and downs of our spiritual "growing up." So essential to our understanding of Julian's theology is the concept of Christ as Mother that I have chosen to quote her at some length on this vital portion of her belief:

> So in our true Mother Jesus our life is founded in his own prescient wisdom from without beginning, with the great power of the Father and the supreme goodness of the Holy Spirit. And in accepting our nature he gave us life, and in his blessed dying on the Cross he bore us to endless life. And since that time, now and ever until the day of judgement, he feeds us and fosters us, just as the great supreme lovingness of motherhood wishes, and as the natural need of childhood asks. Fair and sweet is our heavenly Mother in the sight of our soul, precious and lovely are the children of grace in the sight of our heavenly Mother, with gentleness and meekness and all the lovely virtues which belong to children by nature. For the child does not naturally despair of the mother's love, the child does not naturally rely upon itself, naturally the child loves the mother and either of them the other.

> These, and all others that resemble them, are such fair virtues, with which our heavenly Mother is served and pleased. And I understood no greater stature in this life than childhood, with its feebleness and lack of power and intelligence, until the time that our gracious Mother has brought us up into our Father's bliss. And there it will truly be made known to us what he means in the sweet words when he says: All will be well, and you will see it yourself, that every kind of thing will

be well. And then will the bliss of our motherhood in Christ be to begin anew in the joys of our Father, God, which new beginning will last, newly beginning without end (CW, pp. 304–305; ET, pp. 617–18).

As I have suggested, for Julian our turning toward God involves our turning to Christ. This movement must begin on the cross, with our total sharing of Christ's pain, a sharing that I find most powerful on Good Friday each year as I attempt to join Christ on the cross for those three hours and try to feel as he felt in his betrayal, his cruel suffering, and his very death. For we cannot expect to share in Easter Sunday's resurrection if we have not shared in the full horror of Good Friday's events. Conversely, the more we are able to share in Christ's Passion, the greater will be our joy at his victory over sin and death in his resurrection. Julian's visions were all made clear to her within the context of her sharing vividly in Christ's agony:

> This revelation of Christ's pains filled me full of pains, for I know well that he suffered only once, but it was his will now to show it to me and fill me with mind of it, as I had asked before. And in this time that Christ was present to me, I felt no pain except for Christ's pains; and then it came to me that I had little known what pain it was that I had asked, and like a wretch I regretted it, thinking that if I had known what it had been, I should have been reluctant to ask for it. For it seemed to me that my pains exceeded any mortal death. I thought: Is there any pain in hell like this pain? (CW, p. 209; ET, pp. 364–65).

For Julian, this sharing of the pain of Christ is an ontological bond between herself and Christ. The profound difference she enunciates is that for the Christian it is not sufficient to stand at the foot of the cross, but we must be nailed through our own experience of pain to that very cross in our sharing of his agony. Our failure to be united to Christ in his suffering can only cause him further pain. This does not mean that Christ's sacrifice and death were insufficient for our salvation, but that we will comprehend the fullness of his gift to us only by being entirely present throughout the process of Christ's gift to us.

The crucifixion stands as the greatest example of sin, as alienation from God and God's love for us, and it remains scandalous to us that Christ who was without sin should die for all of us, sinners:

For he who is highest and most honorable was most foully brought low, most utterly despised; for the most important point to apprehend in his Passion is to meditate and come to see that he who suffered is God, and then to consider two lesser particulars. One is what he suffered; the other is for whom he suffered (CW, p. 213; ET, pp. 374–75).

As we meditate on these things, we need to share in Julian's detailed vision of the crucifixion, not as standing beneath the cross, then, but as sharing fully with Christ the experience of being on the cross itself. Only then can we grasp the complete union of God to humanity in Christ, rather than avoiding this understanding by denying Christ's humanity and thus our ability to share in his suffering. Christ's sacrifice is all-sufficient:

> The precious plenty of his precious blood overflows all the earth, and it is ready to wash from their sins all creatures who are, have been and will be of good will (CW, p. 200; ET, pp.344-45).

> With a kindly countenance our good Lord looked into his side, and he gazed with joy, and with his sweet regard he drew his creature's understanding into his side by the same wound; and there he revealed a fair and delectable place, large enough for all mankind that will be saved and will rest in peace and love. And with that he brought to mind the dear and precious blood and water which he suffered to be shed for love. And in this sweet sight he showed his blessed heart split in two, and as he rejoiced he showed to my understanding a part of his blessed divinity, as much as was his will at that time, strengthening my poor soul to understand what can be said, that is the endless love which was without beginning and is and always shall be.

> And with this our good Lord said most joyfully: See how I love you . . . (CW, pp. 220–21; ET, pp. 394–95).

We will gain salvation through our compassionate suffering with Christ, a salvation through love in spite of sin, since God accomplishes all things through this love, which is capable of healing all and any pain. God knows when the healing is needed, because God undergoes any suffering that his creatures encounter and that his creatures cause through their continuing sinning. In spite of this presence of sin and evil, God accomplishes all things in his love. God experiences all things that we experience, and when we weep, God weeps with us. But God turns our falling and our pain to our own good, by being present to us in our falling and pain. God is to be found in the cancer ward, at the deathbed, in the tragedies that surround us. Sin and evil are incapable of destroying God's love for us, and God will not permit us to suffer beyond what we can endure. This fact leads to Julian's and our grounds for essential, basic optimism. Our suffering must be seen as a reflection of Christ's suffering, and in this we can rejoice because it brings with it the promise of our sharing in Christ's resurrection, for "as in Adam all [men] die, even so in Christ shall all be made alive" (*Book of Common Prayer*, p. 46).

It is in the relationship between God, Christ, and Adam that Julian confirms her faith in our resurrection and salvation from this world of sin, expressed in her parable of the Lord and the Servant. This parable contains themes similiar to those in the Suffering Servant of Second Isaiah and the vision of Ezekiel, in that her servant represents both Adam (or humanity) and Christ, once again reflecting the dual nature of Christ as being both fully human and at the same time completely divine:

> In the servant is comprehended the second person of the Trinity, and in the servant is comprehended Adam, that is to say all men. And therefore when I say "the Son," that means the divinity which is equal to the Father, and when I say "the servant," that means Christ's humanity, which is the true Adam. By the closeness of the servant is understood the Son, and by his standing to the left is understood Adam. The lord is God the Father, the servant is the Son, Jesus Christ, the Holy Spirit is the equal love which is in them both. When Adam fell, God's Son fell; because of the true union which was made in heaven, God's Son could not be separated from Adam, for by Adam I understand all mankind. Adam fell from life to death, into the valley of this wretched world, and after that into hell. God's Son fell with Adam, into the valley of the womb of the maiden who was the fairest daughter of Adam, and that was to excuse Adam from blame in heaven and on earth; and powerfully he brought him out of hell. By the wisdom and the goodness which were in the servant is understood God's Son, by the poor laborer's clothing and standing close by on the left is understood Adam's humanity with all the harm and weakness which follow. For in all this our good Lord showed his own Son and Adam as only one man. The

strength and goodness that we have is from Jesus Christ, the weakness and blindness that we have is from Adam, which two were shown in the servant.

And so has our good Lord taken upon him all our blame; and therefore our Father may not, does not wish to assign more blame to us than to his own beloved Son Jesus Christ (CW, pp. 274–75; ET. pp.532–34).

We shall be taking a fuller look at Julian's parable of the Lord and the Servant in the chapter on Julian's theology of sin and redemption. Here it becomes clear that for Julian, Christ is identified fully with the servant as with Adam, and in both instances she is underlining Christ's fully human nature, as complete as his divinity. This passage also reminds us of the intention of the Creator God to redeem humanity through his Son, as Julian states it at another point:

He who created man for love, by the same love wanted to restore man to the same blessedness and to even more (CW, p.194; ET, pp. 329–30).

Once again, Christ's saving role cannot be separated from his role as the church, whose existence must depend on its ability to be a channel for humanity's salvation. Julian is convinced that, much as the church is shaken and tossed, it will remain unbroken, in that it is God's creation and is personified in Christ. If Christ is the church, then the church is where we go to be fed by Christ our Mother, in the eucharist, and the church is literally our spiritual home, to which we return whenever we need the support, help, and comfort of our Mother Christ. The church could have survived only if this were true, because of God's presence in it, through Christ, because, as I have already suggested, for Julian, the church is Christ, because he dwells in it and created it out of his love. Thus, to turn to the church is to turn to Christ and thus receive God himself in our lives. Given this role in Julian's perception of the church and her identification of Christ so completely with the church, it is not surprising that Julian requires loyalty to "Mother Church" as a sine qua non of our faith.

Just as our identification with Christ, and most particularly his Passion, are at the very core of Julian's theology, so is the resurrection a constant theme in her thinking. For, as we all die in Adam, just as important, we are all made alive in Jesus Christ in the true life. For Julian the true life is the life hereafter, when we fully take up our divine substance or being, "oned" to God. Death, therefore, to Julian, comes as a great blessing:

> Suddenly you will be taken out of all your pain, all your sickness, all your unrest and all your woe. And you will come up above, and you will be filled full of joy and bliss, and you will never again have any kind of pain, any kind of sickness, any kind of displeasure, no lack of will, but always joy and bliss without end (CW, p. 306; ET, pp. 620–21).

Here Julian shares the vision of those familiar resurrection passages of Romans 8, 1 Corinthians 15, and Revelation 21, in which we can look forward to our "endless bliss," joined to our Lord God who will "reign in his house as a king and fill it all full of joy and mirth, gladdening and consoling his dear friends with himself, very familiarly and courteously, with wonderful melody in endless love in his own fair blissful countenance, which glorious countenance fills all heaven full of joy and bliss of the divinity" (CW, p. 203; ET, pp. 351-52). Heaven is no solemn affair for Julian, but is suffused with joy, bliss and the same laughter which she shared with Christ during her revelations: "For I understood that we may laugh, to comfort ourselves and rejoice in God, because the devil is overcome" (CW, p. 202; ET, p. 349).

The heavenly banquet is an occasion of continuous praise, being beyond the restrictions of time and space, fed by the joy of final victory over the devil and death itself. For Julian it also connotes that time when the great secret will be revealed to us. Julian is not told what God's "great deed" will be, but she is assured that there will be such a deed. She accepts this assurance on account of her deep conviction of the total love of God for us, who looks upon us, in all our sinfulness, "with pity, not with blame." We are not told, any more than Julian was told, what this great deed will be, but my faith suggests that the great deed, which none of us can comprehend in this life, will be the fact of our personal resurrection. Our eventual understanding of this will lead to Julian's "three degrees of bliss," in which we will receive worship and thanks; we will see the worship and thanks experienced by all; and this worship and thanks will be endless, resulting in Julian's "five joys": rejoicing, praise, thanksgiving, love, and blessedness, a state to which all of us can look forward with the same joy and optimism that Julian consistently displayed.

Holy Spirit as Fulfiller

> And so in our making, God almighty is our loving Father, and
> God all wisdom is our loving Mother, with the love and good-
> ness of the Holy Spirit, which is all one God, one Lord (CW,
> p. 293; ET, pp. 582–83).

Julian perhaps says less about the Holy Spirit directly in her
Revelations than she says of the other two persons of the Trinity.
This I believe is not so much because she holds the Holy Spirit in
less high regard, but because the entire work and her whole life
are totally suffused by the Holy Spirit, to the extent that her
adoption by the Holy Spirit is a self-evident fact of her very existence. For Julian, the divine love that is expressed by the actions
of the Holy Spirit is not just a feeling or one of the attributes of
the Trinity, but a total relationship in which we are called to be
indwelling in the Trinity. It is the Holy Spirit who moves the
indwelling, divine love of Christ in our souls, just as the Holy
Spirit moves within the Trinity in an action known as
perichoresis, which means "moving around, yet remaining all one
piece." The Holy Spirit's job is, then, to move around among us,
holding us together as one piece, and at the same time complet-
ing, unifying, and fulfilling our God-given destinies.

As has already been noted, Julian prayed for three "wounds of
the Spirit," which for her were contrition, compassion, and a
longing for God. These she wished to experience through a bodily sight or corporeal vision; through her desire to suffer fully
with Christ; and through a desire to share in Christ's dread:

> I wanted to have every kind of pain, bodily and spiritual,
> which I should have if I had died, every fear and temptation
> from devils, and every other kind of pain except the departure
> of the spirit (CW, p. 178; ET, p. 287).

For Julian, the spiritual experience of sharing in Christ's crucifixion as fully as possible was the necessary prerequisite to sharing in the fullness of his resurrection. Julian saw the three
wounds as her way to be fulfilled in the Spirit. She enunciates
other important works of the Spirit. Prayer is the work of the
Spirit, a two-way relationship between God and humanity in
which listening to God is every bit as important as talking at
God. We listen to God by listening to our Lord, Christ. The Holy
Spirit also works among us as an agent for the disposal of sin and
blame. The Holy Spirit is, as it were, the cleaning agent that gives
us our fresh start, wiping out all our past sins, omissions, and

failures. The Holy Spirit is our principal weapon in our struggle
with demonic oppression and the wiles of the devil, all the testing and temptation that we daily face in our lives in this imper-
fect world. The Holy Spirit is the vehicle of our faith and the
energy within the sacraments which form the nucleus of the
church's work and daily existence. Thus the Holy Spirit deter-
mines the nature of the church, while in no way detracting from
the church's nature as the embodiment of Christ. The Holy Spirit
is as well the perfect antidote to our fears and anxieties, our
doubts and questions, our moments of unbelief and lapses in our
faith. If we can but trust that God knows how we feel and think,
that God will send us the Holy Spirit to build up our confidence,
give us strength to face whatever confronts us, and stay with us
through the thick and thin of our struggles, we will then know
that this Holy Spirit is boundless in power and ability to sustain
us. Julian sees these actions of the Holy Spirit as the continuing
"oneing" of us to God by the Holy Spirit, the bringing of us to
God, in Christ, which is thus seen as the united action of the
Holy Trinity.

The third form of "charity," charity given, is our response to
God's love, in the Holy Spirit. This can be seen as the expression
of divine love in human beings: how we behave to one another,
the actions we take, the very ways in which we conduct our
lives. If they are modeled on Christ, as God would have it be,
then our lives become the work of the Holy Spirit, examples of
the effectiveness of God's unfailing grace. Julian views our whole
purpose in this life as being available to the actions of the Holy
Spirit, so that we are completed, perfected, and united to God.
We will not experience this fulfillment by the Holy Spirit entirely
in this life, although we are never deprived of the availability of
the Holy Spirit's healing and saving action.

For Julian, the Holy Spirit is that intrinsic part of the Godhead
that was present throughout the "history" of faith, the Spirit that
was present in the Creation and breathed life into this world, the
Spirit that led the children of Israel out of Egypt and inspired the
kings and prophets of old, the Spirit that came upon Christ at his
baptism and remained with him throughout his life, ministry,
passion, death, and resurrection. It is this same Spirit that led the
early church, directed Julian in her life, and still guides us today.
The Holy Spirit is the ultimate force that "ones" us to God in
love. The whole of Julian's *Revelations* is a testament to the Holy
Spirit's unfailing presence and effectiveness.

10

"Oneing"

Together with her orthodox Trinitarian formulation and her Christocentric emphasis, an understanding of Julian's concept of "oneing" is essential to a grasp of her theology overall.

Julian sees oneing as having three facets of its ontological nature. It defines the relationship of God to humanity; it motivates the development of our being in relationship to God's being, and it powers the progression of humanity into the being of God. Oneing is foremost a relationship of joy, for to know God is to know true joy. The act of oneing takes place because God wills us to both know his love and experience his joy, the joy that we will experience in the eternal bliss of the next life. We exist only because of God's love, and God, who created us out of this love, loves us because we are who we are, in spite of what we may think of ourselves. Julian is convinced that God gave her the revelations out of love for her:

> What, do you wish to know your Lord's meaning in this thing? Know it well, love was his meaning. Who reveals it to you? Love. What did he reveal to you? Love. Why does he reveal it to you? For love. Remain in this, and you will know more of the same (CW, p. 342; ET, pp. 732–33).

"Remaining" in God's love describes the condition of being oned to God. Pelphrey defines true oneing thus:

> True oneing, then, is the mutual desire of God for man, and of man for God—which desire comes from God and is met by God's eternal love (Pelphrey, p.149).

God's eternal love, which meets God's desire for us, already exists within us, waiting for us to bring it forth in response to God. This is our essential goodness, shared by God with us, a part of God's creative plan for us, and the force that sustains us in this life—psychologically, physically, and spiritually. This oneing force of love is the only force that can provide our true fulfillment, for, as Julian says:

> Our soul is created to be God's dwelling place, and the dwelling of our soul is God (CW, p. 285; ET, pp. 561–62).

Julian would go so far as to claim that it is in fact easier for the Christian to know God than to know his or her own soul, and that it is only through being oned to God that we begin to learn something about our true selves, which is what God intends us to be. Once we are set on this path of self-knowledge through being oned to God, we find our lives suffused with a calm and a sense of purpose that leads to deep inner joy. We discover our own nature by discovering ourselves in God. The soul is ideally formed to be oned to God, because it is not subject to the restrictions of an earthly nature. It is not bound by the limits of time and space. It is our "substance," in Julian's meaning of that word, which is oned to God. That oneing cannot fail, because in God's eyes our substance has never been separated from God, since before time, or as Julian would say, "from without beginning." So, "greatly ought we to rejoice":

> Greatly ought we to rejoice that God dwells in our soul; and more greatly ought we to rejoice that our soul dwells in God. Our soul is created to be God's dwelling place, and the dwelling of our soul is God, who is uncreated. It is a great understanding to see and know inwardly that God, who is our Creator, dwells in our soul, and it is a far greater understanding to see and know inwardly that our soul, which is created, dwells in God in substance, of which substance, through God, we are what we are.

> And I saw no difference between God and our substance, but, as it were, all God; and still my understanding accepted that our substance is in God, that is to say that God is God, and our substance is a creature of God (CW, p.285; ET, pp. 561–63).

Since our oneing can be seen to be a primary concern in our search for a right relationship with God, it becomes clear that oneing must be one of the principal tasks of the church in any and every age. As Grace Jantzen expresses it:

> It is just this that is the primary task of the Church: mediating the love of God to broken men and women so that they may

find deliverance from their sinfulness and healing for their wounds. . . . The Church's reason for existence is to enable broken human beings to be made whole in the love of God (Jantzen, p. 199).

This insight raises two further elements in our understanding of oneing. First, oneing is not restricted to the individual, but is part of God's plan for all creation. We are oned in community, both the community of the faithful in the church and the community of all our fellow creatures. Oneing is not an exclusive activity for a few chosen; it is for all. Second, oneing is part of the process of healing, itself a process of being made whole—mentally, physically, and spiritually.

Oneing heals three blindnesses, which Julian has identified as our blindness to God's continuous love and care for us, our blindness to our own selfhood and worth in the sight of God, and, because we do not perceive our worth in God's sight, our blindness to our own longing for God and our desire to live in his glory. Oneing is the healing of these blindnesses through Christ. I believe that prayer for healing and the laying-on of hands is another example of God's oneing of himself to us. In this sacrament, as in the reconciliation of a penitent, we are surrendering ourselves once more to God, recognizing that God can do more for us "than either we desire or deserve" (*Book of Common Prayer*, Proper 22, p. 182) and that only God can make us truly whole. Oneing is that act of reconciliation to God that makes healing and wholeness possible, regardless of any physical restraints that we may have to continue to bear. Oneing is not, however, merely the act of being reconciled or healed, it is the very condition of being reconciled and healed.

I have mentioned prayer as part of the process of oneing as healing. Prayer is a major aspect of oneing and one upon which Julian lays considerable emphasis. As suggested in my review of the daily routine of the anchoress, it is probable that Julian spent a minimum of four and a half hours a day in prayer and possibly as long again in meditation each day, year after year. She thus directs us from a wealth of experience we are unlikely to be able to emulate:

Prayer oneth the soul to God, for though the soul may be always like God in nature and in substance restored by grace, it is often unlike him in condition, through sin on man's part. Then prayer is a witness that the soul wills as God wills, and it eases the conscience and fits man for grace. And so he teaches us to pray and to have firm trust that we shall have it; for he beholds us in love, and wants to make us partners in his good will and work. And so he moves us to pray for what it pleases him to do, and for this prayer and good desire which come to us by his gift he will repay us and give us eternal reward (CW, p.253; ET, pp. 475–76).

This passage tells us much about the oneing process. Prayer unites us to God through our souls. While our souls are "substantially" like God and while God restores them continually to his likeness through his grace, our souls are frequently not like God in "condition," on account of our propensity for sin. Prayer reminds us that what our soul really wants is to know the will of God, to will whatever God wills. This was what St. Paul had in mind in encouraging the Philippians to "have that mind in you which is also in Christ Jesus" (2:5) The act of praying to ascertain God's will does two things for us. It sorts out our conscience, making it abundantly clear what is right or wrong in any given circumstance and, most important, it "fits man for grace," another way of saying it prepares us to be oned. As we have already noted, God beholds us in love and ones us to himself for the purpose of making us active in his perfect form of love. Being oned thus propels us to Christian action, for God "wants to make us partners in his good will and work." Prayer will not only one us to God, but will show us that there is work to be done with and for God, and God will tell us what it is that God will have us do. It is, I believe, our fear of hearing what God has in mind for us that prevents many of us from praying or, even if we are praying regularly, prevents us from asking God what God would have us do with our lives. My experience is that if we dare to pray the question, God always has an answer for us. It is often not the answer we hoped for or expected, but when we accept God's plan for us in anything, God always supplies the strength, the will, and the ability to perform the task which God has set us. Not only do we gain enormous immediate satisfaction from being about God's work in whatever way he has determined for each of us, but as Julian states, we have the wonderful knowledge of his promise that "he will repay us and give us eternal reward." We do not act in order to secure this reward, but out of our love for God, a love that God has himself given us. Yet this does not mean that we are prevented from looking forward to this gracious reward with eager anticipation, knowing that the glories that will be revealed are not to be compared with the sufferings of this present time (Romans 8:18).

11

"Three Wounds"

I have already described the three wounds that Julian prayed for—the wounds of contrition, compassion, and true longing for God. Since they formed such an important part of Julian's own process of being oned to God, I believe it is important to focus on these three elements in her theology in somewhat greater detail.

The *Oxford English Dictionary* defines the state of *contrition* as the condition of being "broken in spirit by sense of sin, completely penitent," and points out that the word is derived from a Latin verb which means "to be bruised." In Julian's age, true contrition was seen as a necessary stage toward absolution and satisfaction for sin. I do not believe that this need has been abandoned, but we might today describe it as the need for full awareness of the nature of our sins and a sense of our unworthiness as a result of our sinning and alienation from God. I have already made it clear that Julian neither countenanced nor encouraged wallowing in sin, but that is not to be confused with the acceptance of the reality of our sinful natures. For Julian, contrition often followed forgiveness and even followed the joy she experienced as a result of that forgiveness, a reaction to the overwhelming love that God has displayed for us in the act of forgiving us. This resultant renewed sense of contrition can, I think, be compared to those feelings one experienced as a child following apprehension, admission of guilt, punishment, and then forgiveness by one's parent, on the countless occasions when one was caught in some fell deed. This feeling certainly contained a knowledge that the whole painful process was part of the complicated relationship caused by the parent's love. The parent would not go through the necessary pain were it not for a deep love for the child, comparable to God's love for his creation.

Julian also noted the purging effect of contrition, its help in wiping our spiritual slate clean:

> Sin is the sharpest scourge with which any chosen soul can be struck, which scourge belabors man or woman, and breaks a man, and purges him in his own sight so much that at times he thinks himself that he is not fit for anything but as it were to sink into hell, until contrition seizes him by the inspiration of the Holy Spirit and turns bitterness into hope of God's mercy. And then the wounds begin to heal and the soul to revive, restored to the life of Holy Church. The Holy Spirit leads him to confession, willing to reveal his sins, nakedly and truthfully, with great sorrow and great shame that he has so befouled God's fair image (CW, p.244; ET, pp. 449–50).

Contrition is thus the sorrow we experience when we observe the gap between the model of life to which God calls us, in the humanity of Christ, and the reality of our performance in failing to live up to that model. Contrition also can be seen as part of our response to God's love. As we experience that love, the bruising we feel is like physical bruising, painful, but part of the healing process, part of our transfiguration.

The second of the three wounds, compassion, describes the pity that arises from the sharing of suffering with one who suffers. For Julian, as for the Christian, the ultimate example of compassion is to be found in our sharing of Christ's suffering for all upon the cross, a suffering that continues as Christ shares the pain and despair that we encounter in our lives. At the heart of each of Julian's "shewings" in her *Revelations*, compassion is intertwined with the other two wounds of contrition and the longing for God, and all three wounds operate concurrently. It is explicitly in her experience of the crucifixion itself that Julian is fulfilled in her total sharing ("com-passion") with the sufferings of Christ:

> So was our Lord Jesus afflicted for us; and we all stand in this way of suffering with him, and shall till we come to his bliss (CW, p. 211; ET, p. 369).

Compassion for Christ, according to Julian, leads us toward a compassion for our fellow human beings, most especially for their spiritual—in her terms "substantial"—needs. Once again, compassion, by its very definition, must be shared and cannot be hoarded by the individual. It is essentially compassion for all.

As we feel contrition and compassion, we are inevitably drawn to a deep and true longing for God, part of our experience of being "oned" to God, a longing that becomes a permanent part of our being, not dissimilar to the sense of being in love with another and wishing to spend all our time with him or her. This longing is prompted by the "charity given" which God has implanted in each one of us. It is at this point that faith and charity merge. Our aim is to be conformed to a life of true loving, the loving of God that feels contrition for all persons, sharing in their need for relationship to God, the loving that feels compassion for all persons, sharing in their fears and pain; and the loving that has us praying that all will be joined in our longing for God. For there can be no faith without this kind of loving; there can be none of this kind of loving without faith; and only in relationship to God can either exist. We can love only if we are loved by God. True longing for God is a choice we can make of our own free will, and yet even that longing is a free gift from God.

Thus it can be seen that Julian's "three wounds" lie at the very heart of our understanding of her theology. They point to the direction we must take, should we wish to follow her in her pursuit of total identification with the person of Christ, a pursuit to which I firmly believe we are called, and the basis of Julian's importance to us today.

12

Sin and Redemption

Julian found sin to be the great challenge to her theological understanding. She had difficulty in believing that an all-powerful Creator-God would allow sin to exist. The question of the origin and meaning of sin runs through her entire *Revelations* and it is important to dwell for a while on this preoccupation of Julian's:

> And so in my folly before this time I often wondered why, through the great prescient wisdom of God, the beginning of sin was not prevented. For then it seemed to me that all would have been well (CW, p. 224; ET, p. 404).

Julian looks at the Creation for an understanding of this phenomenon. For, if the Creation was the result of God's self-giving love and if God is immanent in all creation, why are not all things created good? Julian's answer to this question is that through his own self-limitation, God gave us the freedom of choice between good and evil, a choice that was part of God's gracious gift to us and that separates us from lower forms of life. It is this freedom of choice that leads to our sinning and abuse of God's creation. Our faith is then tested by all the evil we encounter in this world, but Julian understands that in spite of what may appear to be a hopeless situation from our point of view, all will be well:

> See, I am God. See, I am in all things. See, I do all things. See, I never remove my hands from my works, nor ever shall without end. See, I guide all things to the end that I ordain them for, before time began, with the same power and wisdom and love with which I made them; how should anything be amiss? (CW, p. 199; ET, pp. 340–41).

Julian tells us to trust such a God, that sin will be overcome, however great the contrary possibility appears to us. We have to accept the Fall and even to view it as a necessary prelude to our redemption. The Fall makes the suffering and the self-offering of the Servant, Christ, both necessary and possible. Christ's suffering, death, and Passion make his resurrection possible and thus ensure the resurrection of Adam and, by extension, all humanity. Not that sinlessness is to be thought of as a bad thing, but God has special love for those of his creatures who have fallen, which happily includes every human being.

Julian confronts her questioning of the nature of sin with the answer she received in her visions, the parable of the Lord and the Servant, which she freely admits it took her twenty years to begin to understand. This parable was, for her, God's answer to the question, "Why do we go on sinning?"

We may recall that in the parable, Julian sees a great lord, clothed in the sky and seated on a throne. The throne is in a desert, and a ragged servant stands before it. The servant turns to perform an errand for his lord and falls into a chasm, from which he cannot rise. The lord lifts the servant from the chasm, and the peasant is immediately transfigured. He is clothed in a shining robe and stands at the right hand of the lord.

During his period in the chasm or ditch, the servant suffers "seven great pains":

> The first was the severe bruising which he took in his fall, which gave him great pain. The second was the clumsiness of his body. The third was the weakness which followed these two. The fourth was that he was blinded in his reason and perplexed in his mind, so much so that he had almost forgotten his own love. The fifth was that he could not rise. The sixth was the pain most astonishing to me, and that was that he lay alone. I looked all around and searched, and far and near, high and low, I saw no help for him. The seventh was that the place in which he lay was narrow and comfortless and distressful (CW, pp. 267–68; ET, pp. 515–16).

The servant is not blamed for falling into the chasm and has not earned the pains that he suffers. In this, the parallel with the Suffering Servant of Second Isaiah is strong. Julian sees that the reward for the servant will be far greater than if he had not fallen into the chasm. Indeed, his wounds will be turned into "high, surpassing honor and endless bliss."

Julian was not wholly clear as to the precise meaning of the parable, even at the time of her composing the Long Version, twenty years after her visions, but the outline was apparent. The lord is God. The servant is Adam, and the servant is also Christ, a joint identification that fits in with Julian's theological understanding, previously discussed. It is the total alienation of the servant that prevents him from recognizing his lord. Julian thus states that it is through our blindness that we are prevented from knowing our own goodness or "God-ness." This leads to despair, guilt and a sense of unworthiness and inability to perceive or receive God's love. But it is at this juncture that God loves us more strongly than ever. If the servant had failed, what then was the task in which he had failed? Julian sees the role of the servant thus:

> He was to be a gardener, digging and ditching and sweating and turning the soil over and over, and to dig deep down, and to water the plants at the proper time. And he was to persevere in his work, and make sweet streams to run, and fine and plenteous fruit to grow, which he was to bring before the lord and serve him with his liking (CW, pp. 273–74; ET, pp. 530–31).

Thus the servant's task was the care of the lord's creation, which care is an act of self-offering love, expressed in toil. It can be seen that this was Adam's task, as well as humanity's, and it was most fully exemplified in the life of Christ. It is appropriate to repeat a substantial portion of Julian's explanation, since it lies at the heart of our understanding of this vital portion of her theological structure:

> In the servant is comprehended the second person of the Trinity, and in the servant is comprehended Adam, that is to say all men. And therefore when I say "the Son," that means the divinity which is equal to the Father, and when I say "the servant," that means Christ's humanity, which is the true Adam. By the closeness of the servant is understood the Son, and by his standing to the left is understood Adam. The lord is God the Father, the servant is the Son, Jesus Christ, the Holy Spirit is the equal love which is in them both. When Adam fell, God's Son fell; because of the true union which was made in heaven, God's Son could not be separated from Adam, for by Adam I understand all mankind. Adam fell from life to death, into the valley of this wretched world, and after that into hell. God's Son fell with Adam, into the valley of the womb of the maiden who was the fairest daughter of Adam, and that was to excuse Adam from blame in heaven and on earth; and powerfully he brought him out of hell. By the wis-

dom and goodness which were in the servant is understood God's Son, by the poor laborer's clothing and the standing close by on the left is understood Adam's humanity with all the harm and weakness which follow. For in all this our good Lord showed his own Son and Adam as only one man. The strength and goodness that we have is from Jesus Christ, the weakness and blindness that we have is from Adam, which two were shown in the servant.

And so has our good Lord Jesus taken upon him all our blame; and therefore our Father may not, does not wish to assign more blame to us than to his own beloved Son Jesus Christ (CW, pp. 274–75; ET, pp. 532–34).

Thus Christ's dual nature, human and divine, is reflected in Adam and also in humanity. Our Lord God's purpose for us is to be transfigured from our human nature, "the weakness and blindness that we have . . . from Adam," to our divine nature, "the strength and goodness that we have . . . from Jesus Christ."
Julian blames sin for our distancing from God:

I saw that nothing hindered me but sin, and I saw that this is true of us all in general, and it seemed to me that if there had been no sin, we should all have been pure and as like our Lord as he created us (CW, p. 224; ET, p.404).

The cause of the Fall, the purpose of sin, for Julian remains a mystery, although she sees that sin presents an opportunity for our salvation. She acknowledges that sin will persist in this life and cautions us not to be too hard on ourselves as a result of this:

But do not be too much aggrieved by the sin which comes to you against your will (CW, p. 338; ET, p. 717).

Indeed, Julian sees a danger in perfectionism, or an unrealistic expectation of ourselves. We can expect to sin, and while we should do everything within our power to avoid sinning, we should not let our continual failing get us down, for each failure presents an opportunity for us to experience God's love for us. Sin is not something God does to us, but rather it is the absence of relationship to God. The pain which we feel in sinning is useful in reminding us of our alienation and recalling us to a right relationship to God. Sin requires compassion, not judgment, both from God for humanity and from humanity for humanity. God sees our sins with pity and not blame. We are therefore called to view those who sin with that same compassion. We are not called to judge others' misdeeds. We can never know the pressures under which they were operating in order to reach the point of doing whatever they have done. If we begin to understand the depth of God's saving love for each one of us, then we will begin to hate sin, which we will come to see as a perversion of our human nature. Both St. Paul and Aquinas share Julian's understanding that God allows evil to happen in order to bring about a greater good and that we will, in spite of our best intentions, continue to do the very evil things we least want to do. As St. Paul so well expressed it in his epistle to the Romans:

> For we know that the law is spiritual; but I am of the flesh, sold into slavery under sin. I do not understand my own actions. For I do not do what I want, but I do the very thing I hate. . . . So I find it to be a law that when I want to do what is good, evil lies close at hand. For I delight in the law of God in my inmost self, but I see in my members another law at war with the law of my mind, making me captive to the law of sin that dwells in my members. Wretched man that I am! Who will rescue me from this body of death? Thanks be to God through Jesus Christ our Lord! (Romans 7:14–25).

Julian also compares sin to sickness in a child, illustrating that God treats the sinner as a parent would a sick child, not disliking the child on account of the sickness, but loving it all the more tenderly, recognizing its need to be restored to full health and brought to its maturity. This shows the need of Christ's role as our Mother.

At its worst, sin is for Julian inhumanity, and the most startling example of this sinful inhumanity is humanity's killing of Christ—not only that it was murder, but that it was completely unjustified and lacking in provocation. Nevertheless, the crucifixion gave God the context in which to show the greatest love of all, the salvation of the human race, God's own creation.

Because Julian sees sin as the absence of relationship, she argues that sin does not in itself have existential being:

> But I did not see sin, for I believe that it has no kind of substance, no share in being, nor can it be recognized except by the pain caused by it. And it seems to me that this pain is something for a time, for it purges and makes us know ourselves and ask for mercy (CW, p. 225; ET, pp. 406–407).

Sin is the opposite of life; thus, when we sin, we can be said to be dying to our real selves. And yet sin is necessary. We need the threat of our moral dying in order to cling to moral living. In some way, only by making mistakes can we find our loving, forgiving God, through the actions of his self-giving Son, who has "taken upon him all our blame."

We will continue to be plagued by our three blindnesses, our inability to see God's continuous love and care for us, our blindness to our own selfhood and worth in the sight of God, and our failure to acknowledge the longing for God that is within us. These blindnesses lead us to a state of anxiety, which Julian suggests is a sinful state. As Pelphrey notes:

> In her [Julian's] view, sin is the condition of being unable to grow into adulthood because of our anxiety. Her observation that impatience and despair (or anxiety in general) are our chief illness is notable for our own society, in which anxiety with its accompanying behavior patterns of suicidal despair, schizophrenia, escapism through drugs, destruction of family structures, motiveless crime, and so on, is looked upon as a major social problem to be faced today (Pelphrey, p. 161).

This understanding is certainly one of the reasons that Julian's theology speaks so vividly to us at this time, and it is my contention that the fourteenth century witnessed a similar degree of anxiety, owing to the forces at work that I described in the earlier chapters of this study.

In an age when penance was taken extremely seriously, Julian addresses the subject by saying that no form of penance was suggested to her in her visions, a statement which must have taken her contemporaries by surprise. She suggests that such penance as we undergo is to be found in the pain and suffering which we experience in this life:

> And then you will truly see that all your life is profitable penance.

> This place is prison, this life is penance, and he wants us to rejoice in the remedy. The remedy is that our Lord is with us, protecting us and leading us into the fullness of joy (CW, p. 331; ET, pp. 693–94).

Our self-accusation is useful only if it is effective in turning us to Christ. Julian is strongly opposed to any wallowing in our own sins. Her attitude is all the more remarkable in an age that was obsessed by sin, saw the Black Death as God's punishment, and believed that every possible effort had to be made to avoid long sessions in purgatory paying for one's sinful life. It was this belief that gave indulgences, chantries, and masses for the repose of the dead such popularity, not to mention the more extreme forms of visible penance such as those indulged in by the flagellants.

Julian suggests that all the sin and suffering provide the occasion for the beginning of our return to God. Our pain signals the initiation of our transformation, just as Christ's pain in the crucifixion initiated our salvation. It is one of the great paradoxes of our faith, a scandal, that the greatest display of human wickedness, the crucifixion, was itself the very remedy for that wickedness and the cause of our salvation. As I have already stated, for Julian and for ourselves, Christian belief starts at the cross. In the depth of sin and suffering, we find God's unfailing love, again and again. God is most present in this world's brokenness. It seems that there cannot be good without evil, but we can take courage that there cannot be evil without good. Evil is good gone wrong, and for Julian it has no independent existence, being a negative force—the absence of good.

As our salvation arises from God's action in the midst of sin and evil, so we cannot experience any suffering without also being aware of the potential joy that accompanies God's transformation of the situation. This joy mirrors the joy that Christ felt at his suffering on behalf of our salvation:

> [It is] . . . so great a joy to Jesus that he counts as nothing his labor and his sufferings and his cruel and shameful death. . . . This deed and this work for our salvation were as well devised as God could devise it. It was done as honorably as Christ could do it, and here I saw complete joy in Christ, for his joy would not have been complete if the deed could have been done any better than it was (CW, pp. 217–18; ET, pp. 384–88).

As with Jesus, the pain that we bear is directly related to the reward we shall receive. Through our pain we develop the three wounds of contrition, compassion, and true longing for God, without which we would not be receptive to God's love. Julian points out that many of the great saints of the church provide fine examples of the power of God's transforming love. The glimpses we are given of heaven assure us that the suffering and pain of this life are not in vain, are not to be compared, as St. Paul tells the Romans, with the glories that shall be revealed to us (Romans 8:18). We are reminded that the greatest suffering of all time, that of Jesus on the cross, ended in the joy of Easter morning.

Julian describes life as one of continual falling and rising, an experience we might describe today as the "roller coaster of life."

The traditional description of the spiritual journey tends to define a linear progression up some ladder or scale, as in Walter Hilton's *Scale of Perfection*, a hierarchical view of spiritual improvement seen also in Langland's *Piers Ploughman*, with Dowel (Do-well), Dobet (Do-better) and Dobest (Do-best), reflecting three grades of spiritual proficiency: beginner, proficient, and perfect. Julian would have accepted the three stages of purgation, illumination, and union with God, but my sense is that she saw this life as an ongoing up and down motion toward our goal. Julian never refers to a ladder or an ascent. She does not even refer to stages in the contemplative life, and there are no references to particular ascetical practices in her *Revelations*, which are marked throughout with a fine tone of moderation in spiritual matters. I believe this is because Julian saw no hierarchical structure in the Christian economy: all souls are equal in God's eyes and our spiritual efficiency is not to be measured against that of our "even-Christians." This attitude is further evidence of the unlikelihood of Julian's membership in a monastic order of nuns, for whom hierarchy tends to be an ever-present reality. For Julian, the ups and downs, the "roller coaster of life," are all part of our ultimate transfiguration. This transfiguration is achieved in that our sin is replaced by God's love. The pain of sin is necessary to our growth and healing, but this pain is overcome by love, not by retribution. Indeed, God chooses real sinners to become saints. Julian selects some prime examples of this process, including Mary Magdalene, Peter, Paul, Thomas of India, and John of Beverly. Julian confirms Christ's message that he came to call not the righteous, but sinners to repentance. Thus, for God and for the recipient, the greater the sinner, the greater the joy in healing. But Julian does not fall into the trap of antinomianism, whereby we are encouraged to sin the more so as to receive greater salvation, a heresy tackled by St. Paul in his epistle to the Romans:

> What then are we to say? Should we continue in sin in order that grace may abound? By no means! (Romans 6:1–2).

Rather, we are called to become as like Christ as we can, because we not only do we have the innate ability to do so, but that power of becoming like Christ is already at work within us, even when we do not realize it. We move from separation from God to communion with God, and we do this by sharing in Christ's transfiguration, which Julian observed on the cross itself:

Suddenly, as I looked at the same cross, he changed to an appearance of joy. The change in his appearance changed mine, and I was as glad and joyful as I could possibly be (CW, pp. 214–15; ET, p. 379).

This transfiguration from pain to joy is none other than a transfiguration from death to life, our participation in the full resurrection event of Easter. We, like Christ, are changed by the cross. Evil and death are overcome, although we will continue to be accosted by the devil in our fears and nightmares, as Julian was in her vision of "the Fiend." The fiend attempted to assault Julian physically during her revelations, seeking to do actual physical violence to her and trying to lead her to despair by showing her her guilt. Julian is perhaps less impressed with the devil's more obvious forms of temptation, those well-known mortal sins of lechery, gluttony, sloth, and so on. For her, and for all of us, I suspect, the devil's cunning is much more dangerous when he is trading in despair, guilt, anxiety, and apathy, using the more dramatic and evident vices as a "smoke screen" behind which to operate. Julian's attack by the devil seems to me to personify a potential crisis of faith, coming at the end of all her visions, the awful possibility that the whole matter was a hallucination, that her revelations were one almighty hoax, the unthinkable horror of contemplating the idea that God does not exist—a temptation that assaults each of us daily. However, once stared directly in the face and confronted with God's love, these temptations serve only to turn us more strongly than ever toward God.

The reason that we need not fear, whatever "the Fiend" attempts upon us, is that we have an eschatalogical secret, having to do with how it is that God will indeed make all things well. Thomas Merton writes wonderfully of his discovery of this secret, in a passage that led me to discover Julian of Norwich for myself:

> I pray much to have a wise heart, and perhaps the rediscovery of Lady Julian of Norwich will help me. . . . She is a true theologian with greater clarity, depth and order than St. Teresa: she really elaborates, theologically, the content of her revelations. . . . One of her most telling and central convictions is her orientation to what one might call an eschatalogical secret, the hidden dynamism which is at work already and by which "all manner of thing shall be well." This "secret," this act which the Lord keeps hidden, is really the fruit of the Parousia. It is not just that "He comes," but He comes with the

secret to reveal, He comes with the final answer to all the world's anguish, this answer which is already decided, but which we cannot discover and which, (since we think we have reasoned it all out anyway) we have stopped trying to discover (Merton, pp. 191–92).

This eschatalogical transfiguration is not earned, but is the free gift of God to God's creation, through God's own Son. Guilty, we are set free. Julian's complete grasp of justification by faith sets her apart from most of her contemporaries who were much absorbed in justification through works, as the fifty-six churches in Norwich in her day might attest. Her strongly Pauline stance in this area places her theology in line with that of the early church and has her anticipating the theology of Martin Luther and the Reformers, two hundred years ahead of their time. It can also be stated that her theology of sin and redemption finds her at her most Anglican and further explains her growing popularity with current Anglicans the world over. She speaks, however, to all, although she avoids universalism by restricting redemption to "those who will be saved" (CW, p. 326; ET, p. 680).

It is not clear whom Julian would exclude from God's saving action, and yet it is evident that not all will receive it. The distinction is not made on the basis of sin, for:

God has made things to be loved by men and women who have been sinners (CW, p. 167; ET, p. 272).

For me, there is little doubt that the great secret has to do with how God redeems the entire creation. This act, the magnitude of which we are unable to grasp, was made possible by the sufficiency of Christ's sacrifice for us, whose mothering action will bring us, his children, to our full maturity in the Spirit, our final "oneing" in the Trinitarian Godhead.

Since we have already been saved, redeemed from our sins, we shall now be able to comprehend the way in which God's judgment differs from the judgment of this world.

13

God's Judgment

Julian's understanding of God's judgment, as has been suggested, closely parallels that of St. Paul, although, if anything, she takes the concept of justification by faith further than he does. This doctrine declares that in spite of our sinful actions and deeds, we will be judged according to our faith, a faith that includes the belief that faith is what allows us to be forgiven. Thus, in a courtroom metaphor, when we are called before Christ our judge, we shall hear the charges, most of which will be sins of attitude rather than immoral actions. To these we will plead guilty, expressing our sorrow and contrition. At which point, Christ our judge will pronounce us guilty and inform us that our sentence is to go free, since we are not blamed for what we have done, merely pitied for what we have had to suffer on account of these sins. In this radical way does heavenly justice differ from earthly justice.

The sins we commit are caused by the lack of integration between our substantial and sensual selves, for which we are in part to blame, but for which God does not blame us. In the substitutional theory, popular in the Middle Ages, Christ was deemed to have assumed the blame on our behalf. Julian does not accept this, proposing that God replaces blame entirely with compassion and pity. The church's task is to adopt God's attitude in dealing with the sinner and to replace judgment with compassion. Since God does not impute blame, it is also understood that God feels no anger toward the sinner:

> And so in all this contemplation it seemed to me that it was necessary to see and know that we are sinners and commit many evil deeds which we ought to forsake, and leave many good deeds undone which we ought to do, so that we deserve

pain, blame and wrath. And despite all this, I saw truly that our Lord was never angry, and never will be. Because he is God, he is good, he is truth, he is love, he is peace; and his power, his wisdom, his charity and his unity do not allow him to be angry. For I saw truly that it is against the property of his power to be angry, and against the property of his wisdom and against the property of his goodness. God is that goodness which cannot be angry, for God is nothing but goodness. Our soul is united to him who is unchangeable goodness. And between God and our soul there is neither wrath nor forgiveness in his sight. For our soul is so wholly united to God, through his own goodness, that between God and our soul nothing can interpose (CW, p. 259; ET, pp. 492–93).

God's judgment is the judgment of his Son, Christ, a judgment based completely on love, and in this way totally distinct from the judgment and justice of the world we know. Julian sees God's justice as a saving and not a punishing justice, part of the process of being oned to God in our progression to paradise:

Our good Lord protects us with the greatest loving care when it seems to us that we are almost forsaken and abandoned because of our sins and because we see that we have deserved it. And because of the meekness that we obtain from this, we are raised very high in God's sight by his grace. And also God in his special grace visits whom he will with such great contrition, and also with compassion and true longing for him, that they are suddenly delivered from sin and pain, and taken up into bliss and made equal with the saints. By contrition we are made clean, by compassion we are made ready, and by true longing for God we are made worthy. These are the three means, as I understand, through which all souls come to heaven, those, that is to say, who have been sinners on earth and will be saved (CW, pp. 244–45; ET, pp. 451–52).

Unlike the world's judgment, God's judgment is eternally consistent, being based on an unquenchable love for all created beings, no matter what they have thought, said, or done. As a result of this total love, there is a sense in which there is no forgiveness with God, because forgiveness presupposes blame, as quoted above:

And between God and our soul there is neither wrath nor forgiveness in his sight (CW, p. 259; ET, p. 493).

This all ties in with Julian's concept, which is entirely orthodox, whereby we have already been saved by Christ's offering of
himself upon the cross, "a full, perfect and sufficient sacrifice,
oblation and satisfaction, for the sins of the whole world" (*Book
of Common Prayer*, p. 334). That this has indeed already taken
place is further evidence of the timelessness of God's judgment,
or "non-judgment."

Julian, then, in defining the judgment of God, shifts the
emphasis from worldly judgment, punishment, and dread to
heavenly justice, love, healing, and reconciliation to God.

A Definition of Hell

Julian requested a vision of hell and purgatory during her
visions. This request was not granted, for reasons which I believe
become apparent as we look at Julian's theology concerning hell.
Hell, in Julian's terms, is a state into which we can fall in this life.
Hell is none other than our alienation from God, the product of
our sinning, a choice we are able to make given our gift from
God of the freedom of choice. Total alienation from God, a complete unawareness of the existence of God, leads to a state in
which we have no future beyond this life, or, at best, in which
we face a future of complete nothingness. This prospect can only
lead us to despair, which means literally, from its French deriva-
tion, the "absence of hope." This would place one in a situation
where one was, through one's own choice, beyond the reach of
God's caring love, so possessed by evil as to be unavailable for
God's saving action. Julian accepts this awful possibility:

> By this sight I understand that every creature who is of the
> devil's condition in this life and so dies is no more mentioned
> before God and all his saints than is the devil, notwithstand-
> ing that they belong to the human race (CW, p. 234; ET, pp.
> 427–28).

Thus, hell is a place in which we choose to be absent from
God, not a place to which God consigns us as a punishment. I
would still maintain that such a place is one that we may choose
to inhabit in this life. I am not convinced that a loving, merciful
God would allow any of creation to choose such a place as an
eternal state. To accept that such a place could exist in a future
life would be to accept that God does indeed punish us for our
misdeeds. This concept is alien to Julian's theology. Could it
therefore be that the reason God did not show Julian a vision of

hell and purgatory was that it was already available for her inspection all around her, as it surrounds us today? We have only to see the actions of which humanity is capable to begin to grasp the strength of this argument. What further illustration of hell is needed in an age that has witnessed the Holocaust? Was not the crucifixion itself the ultimate example of hell on earth? Could not the greatest hell be the very fear of such situations and events, the worst of which is still capable of God's transformation? A denial of God's ability to transform even these horrendous situations becomes a denial of the power of God itself. Julian acknowledges the power of fear in our lives and describes four kinds of "dreads" or fears: the fear that comes from our weakness, the fear of pain or torment, the fear of doubt or anxiety that leads to despair, and reverent fear, the only fear that is divinely inspired and is akin to the awe which God's presence in our lives precipitates. The first three fears come from our alienation from God and convey a presence of an underlying fear of the hell that has just been described, the hell of becoming isolated from God and God's love for us.

It is my contention that the "great secret," the "great deed," which is not imparted to Julian, nor to ourselves, is that action by which God prevents any of his creation from experiencing hell beyond this life. This power is beyond our comprehension. We are not meant to understand it in this life, for the simple reason that such knowledge would remove even our reverent dread. Because we are human, we would then consistently choose evil over good, being subject to our baser instincts and freed from the conscience that keeps us on the side of good. If we lived with the certainty of our salvation assured, we would lose any motivation toward good or God, a condition that could not fulfill the purpose of our creation.

Julian's understanding of hell, in profound distinction to the visions prevalent in her day, is one of the principal causes of the optimism that surrounds her theology. This is an optimism that has only recently returned to some portions of God's church and that is still sadly absent from many Christian dogmas. That her interpretation holds validity seems to me to spring from its serious acceptance of God's promise of our sure and certain resurrection, through Christ's sacrifice for all.

14

Julian's Theology of Prayer

In examining Julian's contribution to our understanding of prayer, we would do well to recall that in this area she was an expert, spending no less than four and a half hours each day in formal prayer and considerable further time in private prayer and meditation. It is thus not surprising that she has much to contribute. The whole of her *Revelations* has the sense of being a prayer, and I have found passages from it to be useful in my own personal devotions. For Julian, life was prayer and prayer was life. She saw the uniting of everything she did to God as the purpose of her existence, and this process began, continued and ended in prayer. Her whole theology might be summarized in the one phrase: "Prayer oneth the soul to God" (CW, p. 253; ET, p. 475)

As I have mentioned, Julian felt that prayer was best addressed directly to God, rather than through intermediaries such as the saints. This did not preclude prayer through Christ, who was God incarnate. Julian explained that God was "homely" with us, so that we need have no fear of approaching him in prayer. She added that God was the source of all our needs, so that there was little point in directing our prayers elsewhere, and that we can speak freely to God, because he already knows our needs and has already given himself for us and to us, in order to supply those needs.

Julian divides prayer into three categories, but does not see them as having rigid borders. One type of prayer can lead to another and they often overlap. The three forms of prayer are "kind yearning," "beholding," and "thanksgiving." We might today call the first two petition and contemplation, and we would include prayer of praise in the category of thanksgiving.

Julian also describes petitionary prayer as prayer of "beseeching." She suggests that petitionary prayer, as all prayer, while we form it, actually comes from God, who places our petitions within us through the action of the Holy Spirit. Thus prayer comes from God and returns to God. The needs we enunciate are met only by God, and God himself is the object of all our needs. We can therefore ask God for anything, although the response may not be the one we might anticipate. Refreshingly, Julian does not prescribe the form for petitionary or any other kind of prayer. There are no prerequisites for prayer, and each individual is encouraged to approach God in the way that suits him or her best. The reason that the form of prayer is not important for Julian is that God answers our prayers not on the basis of their form or literary merit, but because he loves us and knows our needs before we even ask for them. As a result, Julian encourages us to pray boldly, to pray directly to God, and to pray with joy. She tells us not to become dismayed when our prayers feel barren. God has heard them, even when we sense no response, a problem that will be solved in God's time. Julian enunciates four characteristics of petitionary prayer. First, God makes us want to pray. Second, God makes us ask for our needs. Third, we do in fact ask God for our needs. Finally, God fulfills our needs, but in the way God deems appropriate, not necessarily in the manner we expect. Petitionary prayer is a natural part of the spiritual life:

> Beseeching is a true and gracious, enduring will of the soul, united and joined to our Lord's will by the sweet, secret operation of the Holy Spirit (CW, p. 249; ET, p. 463).

Any petition is an opportunity to be conformed to the will of God. Our oneing to God takes place at a conscious level, in that the more we pray consciously, the more we will come to love God and want to do God's will. By praying, we move toward a more intimate relationship with God, turning our lives over to God, consciously imitating Christ, whose whole life was a life of prayer to the Father. To pray is to acknowledge our need for and dependence on God.

In summary, then, in petitionary prayer, God is its source and its destination; such prayer brings joy, not anxiety, and it conforms us to the image of God, which is Christ. Contemplative prayer continues this process.

Contemplative prayer was aptly defined by Julian as prayer of beholding, the function of gazing upon the person of Christ, his face, or a representation of him, as in the crucifix that Julian used during her visions. This form of prayer is traditionally described as *theoria*. While petitionary prayer is initiated by the individual,

although, as has been stated, it originates from God, contemplative prayer begins in God, with our attention firmly fixed on
God, and turns us to seeing ourselves in God, in the light of
God's love. This form of prayer has found its strongest expression
in the Eastern Orthodox tradition, but has gained immense popularity in Western Christendom in recent times, so that we have
begun to recover a part of our spirituality that had thrived in
Julian's day. This form of inner prayer has been described as
"standing with the mind in the heart before God" (see
Kadloubovsky and Palmer, p. 71). In its beginning stages, this
prayer requires our concentration, but after a while the prayer
itself becomes the motivating force. There is a stage of "crossing
over," after which the soul is in God's hands, and one feels the
sense of being united to God; as Julian describes it,

> This makes the soul which so contemplates like to him who is
> contemplated, and unites it in rest and peace by his grace
> (CW, p.314; ET, pp. 644–45).

Contemplative prayer can thus be seen to contain an osmotic
power, as we are silently and passively absorbed into God, surrendering the last elements of our will to God's will. The results
of engaging in this form of prayer are twofold. God shows himself to us in Christ, either as an extraordinary vision, or in the
teaching of the church, and although our attention is fixed on
God, we see ourselves in God, in the light of Christ, and we see
Christ as he dwells within us. We therefore are enabled to see
ourselves living in Christ, which is the purpose of our being and
the only way in which we can see our true selves, as God
intended us to be. As this identification becomes stronger, we
become more able to discern what we are not intended to be and
we see sin for what it is, a perversion of our true selves and the
cause of our alienation from God.

The oneing action of contemplative prayer makes us whole
and heals us, allowing us to gain an appropriate sense of our
relationship to God:

> For of all things, contemplating and loving the Creator makes
> the soul to seem less in its own sight, and fills it full with rev-
> erent fear and true meekness, and with much love for its fel-
> low Christians (CW, p. 187; ET, p. 309).

One of Julian's understandings of contemplative prayer is the
way in which God chooses when, where, and how to be revealed
in this form of prayer. It is difficult for us to thus abandon our

control over the exercise, a control that we tend to expect in all aspects of our life and work. Here, although we must continuously seek God's presence in this form of prayer, we are on God's time and, in a sense, at God's mercy; as Julian expresses it,

> For we are now so blind and so foolish that we can never seek God until the time when he in his goodness shows himself to us (CW, p. 193; ET, p. 325).

Our blindness and foolishness should not, however, deter us from our soul's "constant search":

> And this vision taught me to understand that the soul's constant search pleases God greatly. For it cannot do more than seek, suffer and trust. And this is accomplished in every soul, to whom it is given by the Holy Spirit. And illumination by finding is of the Spirit's special grace, when it is his will. Seeking with faith, hope and love pleases our Lord, and finding pleases the soul and fills it full of joy. And so I was taught to understand that seeking is as good as contemplating, during the time that he wishes to permit the soul to be in labor. It is God's will that we seek on until we see him, for it is through this that he will show himself to us, of his special grace, when it is his will (CW, p. 195; ET, pp. 332–33).

The effort of seeking to be in a state of contemplative prayer with God is itself pleasing to God, who will, when he chooses, reveal himself to us. Thus this prayer consists of both seeking and seeing. We are called to be continuously seeking, but not in an arduous sense. Julian suggests that the seeking have a light touch. We abide in God's love while we are seeking and we trust God, that he will indeed reveal himself to us, thus revealing ourselves to ourselves, as being in Christ and living in the light of God's love, through Christ.

In "beholding," or contemplative, prayer, we are truly oned to Jesus, because we move from our conscious efforts at prayer into a state of simply being with Christ. Words are at this point unnecessary; the purpose of this prayer is to enjoy God in this life so that we might love God more and more. This joyous vision of prayer and a relationship to God provides an insight into the true nature of all prayer. We begin to understand that when prayer is working for us, we do not find God, but God finds us—a finding that can become an ongoing presence in our lives. The emptiness of Holy Saturday is replaced by the fullness of Easter Day. Contemplative prayer becomes the way in which we come to know God intimately, and thus the way in which we come to know ourselves truly, and in that knowledge, we know ourselves to be oned to God.

The natural response to our gaining of these "knowings," as Julian calls them, is one of praise and thanksgiving, her third form of prayer. Indeed, Julian says, "Thanking is a true inward knowing" (CW, p.250; ET, p. 466).

We praise God with ourselves, with what we think and say and do. There is no evidence that Julian was instructed formally in the art of hesychastic prayer, that is prayer of the heart, but I believe that she arrived at this form of prayer without instruction, unaware of its origins, structure, or formal application, but familiar with it through her own experience of prayer, inspired by God and taught by the Holy Spirit. This is reflected in the way in which prayer is interwoven in all that Julian says in her *Revelations*. Her intimate identification with Jesus may or may not have involved actual enunciation of the Jesus prayer. She may have been too busy with her prayers of praise and joy to accommodate this additional discipline, which was not normative within Western spirituality. Certainly, she advocated continuously acknowledging Christ's blessedness:

> For as truly as we shall be in the bliss of God without end, praising and thanking him, so truly have we been in God's prevision loved and known in his endless purpose from without beginning. In this love without beginning he created us . . . but we shall all say with one voice: Lord, blessed may you be, because it is so, it is well (CW, p. 341; ET, pp. 728–29).

Julian sees the prayer of thanksgiving and praise that we raise in this life as a foretaste of our experience of the hereafter. Then we will experience three "degrees of bliss," in which we will receive worship and thanks, we will see the worship and thanks experienced by all, and this worship and thanks will be endless. For Julian, the prayer of thanksgiving consists in entering this state of bliss here on earth, in anticipation of the joy and bliss that is to come. The absence of hierarchical structure, so typical of Julian, is nowhere more evident than in her treatment of the subject of prayer, which she views as a circular movement from petition to contemplation and praise, followed by thanksgiving— although the order is interchangeable. Movement from and to the center of God's love can and does occur continuously, regardless of the form of prayer being performed. This can perhaps be best understood in diagrammatic form, as follows:

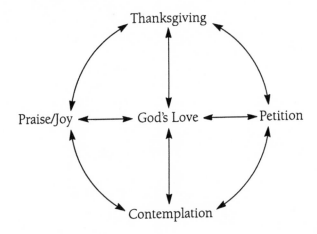

This pattern emerges both from Julian's description of prayer itself and in the format of the *Revelations* themselves, offering us a model of prayer, which becomes as natural to us as breathing and which cannot be separated from anything that we do, as we are oned to God through Christ. In closing this section on Julian's theology of prayer, I offer the prayer from within her text, which sums up so much of what I have been trying to say:

> God, of your goodness give me yourself, for you are enough for me, and I can ask for nothing which is less which can pay you full worship. And if I ask anything which is less, always I am in want; but only in you do I have everything. Amen (CW, p. 184; ET, p. 302).

PART IV
THE MEANING
OF JULIAN
IN OUR TIME

St. Julian Church
Conesford
Norwich, England
as it appears today.

15

A Theology for Today

Julian's theological concerns mirror many of our concerns today. With a world in flux, we seek answers to the questions that faced faithful persons in the fourteenth century. In the light of war, pestilence, and a complete upheaval of the social structure, Julian asks three questions that we ourselves ask. What is the nature and being of God? How does incarnation and atonement affect our lives (or, how does God reach humanity in Christ)? And how does humanity respond to God?

Julian would reply that we need to get back to a right relationship to our God, from whom we have become alienated through our preoccupation with the matters of the world. Her withdrawal from this world into her anchorhold in itself points to a need to withdraw from the pressures that surround us in order to become reconnected to God, through Christ. Yet nowhere does Julian suggest that we are all destined to become anchorites and anchoresses. For Julian, reconnection to God was achieved through mystical experience and prayerful meditation. She does not however claim that we all need to undergo the same mystical experience, in that her experience was given her to share with all people of faith, her "even-Christians."

Nor would it be appropriate to suggest that our world is totally parallel to the world that Julian knew. For all intents and purposes, Julian knew only one church. She would have experienced a plurality of religious orders and even of parishes in Norwich, but there was not the pluralism of faith such as we know it in America today. Muslims were the subject of crusading extermination, rather than a fast-growing segment of the population. Certainly there were sectarian activities, such as those of the Lollards, discussed earlier, but these in no way reflect the inter-denominational and interfaith environment in which the

Christian church operates today. Julian's confidence that only those who believe—and she speaks of those who believe in her faith and her church—will be saved, reflects a lack of charity toward those of other faiths that does not accord with her overall sense of God's unfailing love, reflecting rather the universal attitude of her era. The pluralism that we take for granted did not exist in Julian's time, but this fact does not negate the power of the message that she has to offer us.

Theologically, Julian emphasizes that our faith is based on a Trinitarian and Christological foundation in which unity with God and a total identification with the person of Christ are key elements.

In our need to understand the nature and being of God, we must first be clear concerning the nature of the Trinity, as we experience its activity in our lives. It is this Trinity that created us in the first place, remakes us as it transforms us from our human to our divine nature, or "substance" as Julian would call it, and fulfills us through the power of the Holy Spirit. Julian, particularly strong in her vision of God as Creator, gives us the wonderful image of God holding the world in the palm of God's hand as a hazelnut. She also believes, in common with St. Francis, that God can be found in all creation. She commands us to love this creation with an urgency that fits well with the current concern for the ecological frailty of the world in which we live, a concern heightened by global warming, ozone depletion, and the many other acts of destruction that humanity has visited upon our planet.

Julian's response is that our love for the creation and for each other must echo God's love, which she describes as being reflected in three forms of "charity": uncreated charity, the love within God, evident in the Trinity; created charity, the love of the Trinity for humanity, which we experience through God's presence within us; and charity given, our human response to the love of God, which defines our purpose in life. It is this loving response to which we are called as strongly today as Julian was called those many centuries ago, concisely stated in the summary of the Law: "Thou shalt love the Lord thy God with all thy heart, and with all thy soul, and with all thy mind. This is the first and great commandment. And the second is like unto it: Thou shalt love thy neighbor as thyself" (Book of Common Prayer, p. 324).

In Julian's view, love of God will lead to love of neighbor, because our love of God will lead us to become imitators of Christ. Through concentrating on remaining in a right relationship to God through Christ, Julian assures us, we shall gain three "knowings": knowledge of God, knowledge of ourselves, and knowledge of ourselves as opposed to sin.

We live in a time in which many are searching for their identities, a time of introspection and desire for certainty in an uncertain world environment. Julian suggests that it is through our quest for a knowledge of God that we shall find ourselves, and that this quest is best served by regular and constant communication with our God. Her message points to what we would view as a rigorous spiritual discipline, one that keeps us connected to God through Christ, our "Maker, Keeper, and Everlasting Lover." We will look deeper into the methods that Julian promulgates for this connection when we review her suggestions on methods of prayer, for it is prayer, Julian maintains, that "oneth the soul to God."

As we seek to become oned to God, our principal method is to become at one with Christ, an identification that for Julian was almost total. Julian's strongly Christological approach found its roots in her revelations, in which she shared in Christ's Passion in what was to her a physical way. For her this was consistent with the bodily sickness she suffered and for which she had prayed. Once a year, during Holy Week, Christians tend to concentrate on the suffering and Passion of Christ, with particular emphasis on the rites of Good Friday. Julian would make a strong case for maintaining this intensity throughout the year of Christian devotion, not least as we recall Christ's Passion in the eucharist. For Julian, St. Paul's statements to the Galatians and the Philippians became a living reality:

> I have been crucified with Christ; it is no longer I who live, but Christ who lives in me; and the life I now live in the flesh I live by faith in the Son of God, who loved me and gave himself for me (Galatians 2:20).

> Have this mind among yourselves , which you have in Christ Jesus, who, though he was in the form of God, did not count equality with God a thing to be grasped, but emptied himself, taking the form of a servant, being born in the likeness of men. And being found in human form he humbled himself and became obedient unto death, even death on a cross (Philippians 2:5–8).

Julian sees this Christ, the crucified, suffering Servant, as a model for us all, whether it be as individuals, attempting to live out our lives according to Christ's standards of complete centeredness on God and others, or as a church that is called to be as Christ.

The attempt to live according to the Christ already in us is the challenge that the faithful Christian faces. Julian reminds us of God's immanence within us, that we should seek the Christ where he is to be found within, through prayerful meditation, disciplined prayer, and withdrawal from our hurried daily routines. We can make this time for God without being walled into an anchorhold, but for many of us the achievement of even a modicum of silence in our daily routine seems so hard. We will not be able to engage in Julian's four and a half hours of formal prayer each day, not to mention a further three hours of personal devotions, but we might wish to secure half an hour a day for silent communication with God through Christ.

In his role as church, Christ is, according to Julian, our Father and our Mother and our intimate Lover. Julian is confident that the church will survive, because it is of Christ, while those parts of the institutional church that do not reflect Christ will eventually fail. Julian sees the purpose of the church as one of surrounding its members with the love of Jesus in manifold ways. The church provides the protection of a father, the care and nurture of a mother, and the love we crave as both children and lovers. This church will thus be a living organism, active in three Christ-given areas: doing, knowing, and loving. It is these three activities that form the priorities of a healthy church community, and I would suggest that they can be best understood if placed in the reverse order. It is through our love of God that we shall begin to know God and thus ourselves. As we acquire this dual knowledge, we shall be led to do those actions that God has called us to do, the acts of loving that will be reflected in our pastoral concerns within our community and in acts of outreach to our neighbors in our own community and in the world beyond.

Julian's vivid vision of Christ as Mother is one of her most powerful contributions to our understanding of both Christ's role within our individual lives and the task of the church. For if we are to be not only like Christ, but also in Christ, then we must rediscover the feminine that is within each one of us, so evident in the Christ of the gospel. Hard though this lesson is in the competitive, violent environment we experience at the end of this twentieth century, it is perhaps one of Julian's most significant gifts to us. Here we are not only concerned with the immediate gains to be made in reaching equality for women, within and outside the church, although these gains are important. But beyond full equality for women, Julian's vision speaks to us of a gentleness and compassion for all our fellow creatures, or "even-Christians" as she would term them. She leads us to a nobler, more generous society, which abandons the dog-eat-dog attitude that prevails today. She calls us to imitate the mothering Christ, willing to suffer for her children, with a passionate desire for the healing of those in need and unswervable in her love for her children, regardless of what her children may do to test that love, infinitely trusting and infinitely kind.

Julian thus holds up for us a vision that is in complete contradistinction to the world that surrounds the church, and the church is summoned to model this alternative way of life, to call us back to a right relationship to God in which our base human natures are transformed into our loving souls in Christ, the persons God created us to become. We only begin this process here on earth, but we make that beginning confident that God will complete the process in God's own time. Julian has utter confidence that this transformation is available to us during this life and, indeed, represents the principal purpose of our journey. There is nothing more important to her than our concentration on this loving relationship to God. It takes priority over everything else—a priority that the church today needs to rediscover.

It is the essence of what she calls "oneing," which Julian might well describe as the principal role of the institutional church. Today we might call this the urge for unity, which Christ himself prayed for: "that all might be one, as I and the Father are one," (John 17:22) a condition that should not be confused with church union, since it has become evident through the centuries that God has given us the freedom to worship in the way we choose.

As I stated earlier, oneing becomes a prime task for the institutional church, which is the business of reconciling humanity with humanity and humanity with God, so well expressed by Jantzen:

> It is just this that is the primary task of the Church: mediating the love of God to broken men and women so that they may find deliverance from their sinfulness and healing for their wounds. . . . The Church's reason for existence is to enable broken human beings to be made whole in the love of God (Jantzen, p.199).

The church becomes involved wherever there is need, oppression, injustice, fear, sickness, pain, or despair, not because it is the church's duty, but out of the love that unites us most of all to those who are in greatest need of God's universal love, thereby exhibiting Christ's bias toward the poor and unloved of this world. It is the engaging in this task of love that brings us closer to God's love ourselves, as we experience ourselves freed from the anxieties we felt as we pursued the world's priorities. Just as Julian did not call all to the life of the anchorhold, so it is my conviction that we are not all called to service within the institutional church, but are placed within our secular fields of endeavor to bring that same love to our fellow human beings, wherever we or they may be.

Oneing has three vital characteristics. It is achieved in community; it is inclusive of all; and it is a process of healing, or being made whole. Julian defines it as a cure for three blindnesses: blindness to God's love for us; blindness to our own selfhood; and blindness to our own longing for God.

It seems to me that these blindnesses describe accurately much of the malaise within the church and society today, and that the church's task is to be about the process of "re-oneing" us to God, so that we may rediscover our true natures and live to enjoy our loving relationship to God. This process, Julian insists, is best achieved through our total identification with the person of Christ, through prayer and meditation, which will then lead to appropriate action.

The order of progression mirrors Julian's "three wounds" of contrition, compassion, and desire for God. We are first to experience contrition, to gain an awareness of our alienation from God—in essence to self-diagnose. This process will not only purge us of our un-Godly attitudes, but will help us to gain a realization of God's love for us in spite of our unworthiness. As we shall once more see when we revisit the problems of evil and sin in the world around us today, Julian does not think of sin and evil as having an independent existence, but rather as the absence of relationship to God, expressed as hell when it becomes a total absence or complete alienation from God. The sorrow we feel as part of our contrition arises from our observation of the distance that separates our behavior and the model we are attempting to achieve. Thus the bruising that contrition contains signals the beginning of our self-awareness and the onset of our healing process.

Our compassion must begin with identification with the suffering Christ, as described earlier, which can only lead us to awareness of and identification with the suffering of those around us. We will find our sensitivity heightened and begin to know what it feels like to be in the other person's place, to have a sense of what it really feels like to be homeless, unemployed, hungry, desperate, discriminated against, and unloved. Such sensitivity will lead us to find cures for the causes of these conditions rather than to offer sentimental band-aids, to attack the roots of the evils that surround us. Such evils are, in simple terms, a lack of love and respect for our fellow human beings, those whom Julian would refer to as our "even-Christians," who lie there in the ditch like the servant of Julian's parable, awaiting the transformation that Christ brings them, through us.

It is probable that some will see this interpretation of Julian's theology as too proactive, too heavily retrospective, an attempt to coopt Julian for a contemporary polemic, inasmuch as Julian was not faced with the challenges of twentieth-century America. But I see her call as one that bids us live out the gospel, to become so identified with Christ that we will know what to do and that our actions will spring from this identification with the basic demands of Christian love. And it was to the simple basics of Christianity that Julian called her church.

16

The Challenge of Evil

As stated earlier, Julian acknowledged the world's imperfections, saw the need for contrition and transformation, but did not accept the belief that an evil power existed in competition with God. She saw evil and sin as alienation from God and the absence of God's love. Nevertheless, she admitted that the world she knew was far from having achieved a state of oneness with God and was not naive concerning the evils of her day. Three occurrences of the Black Death, a hundred years of war, famine occasioned by several harvest failures, rebellion and civil strife, as well as extremes of social injustice, all combined to reinforce a sense that even if God and good would eventually triumph, there were still major challenges to be faced—a reason for Julian's plea that the church should keep its own house in order.

As evil and sin did exist, Julian described them as not "of God" and assured her fellow Christians that these forces would not prevail in the long run. She saw God as hating the sin but not the sinner, whom God viewed "with pity, not with blame." A God who identifies with the sinner's plight, rather than standing aloof from it, fits well into a present-day church that is just beginning to recover from a period of heavy judgmentalism. Such judgmentalism reached a climax in the years of Victorian hypocrisy, in which God was seen to favor the "haves" and to condemn all who were not part of the self-elected establishment, whose behavior in private often had little to do with their public postures. Julian prescribes a strict moral discipline and imposes an incredibly high standard of behavior upon the Christian, but nowhere does she suggest that failure to reach such high standards will be visited by a wrathful, vengeance-seeking God. I see no possibility that Julian would have had any sympathy for the rising tide of right-wing fundamentalism that so easily condemns those who are not in line with its particular beliefs and too readily identifies itself as being the saved, to the exclusion of all who do not share such rigid beliefs. Julian sees God's reaction of pity as the correct response to the evil and sin that surrounds us.

Going yet further, Julian would claim that there is no need for forgiveness, as far as God is concerned, since God has already forgiven us in the salvific act of Christ's death for us on the cross. The good news is that we have been saved and forgiven through the timeless act of God's forgiveness, "once for all" (Rom. 6:10). This, however, does not negate our human need to feel forgiven, a state to which we come when we have confessed our sinfulness and received absolution, when our slates have been wiped clean and we are free to begin once again our attempt to lead more Christlike lives.

Julian then asks, "Why do we go on sinning?" She does not receive a direct answer to this prayerful question, but is given as an indirect reply the parable of the Lord and the Servant, which speaks to us of the transformation Christ works for us when we sin. Christ, identified with the Suffering Servant of Isaiah, shared our fallenness and brokenness in identifying himself with the fallen Adam and the Passover victim. Just as Christ was himself raised up by God from the Cross, so we are raised up to salvation from our sins and death by the saving action of Christ.

We are not invited to fall into the trap of sinning all the more in order to receive greater forgiveness, but we are urged to oppose evil in all its forms, since it prevents us from being in a right relationship to God.

Julian explains the existence of evil as a result of God's self-limitation, made necessary by God's gift to humanity of the freedom of choice. In other words, if God had created us perfect, we would have no freedom of choice in either thought, word, or deed. This is a costly but priceless freedom. It allows us to choose between good and evil, to experience the distinction between hell and heaven and thus gain intimations of what paradise holds in store for us, a state in which there will be total union with God and the complete absence of pain, suffering, and alienation from God. This is the costly freedom that prevents God from interfering with us even when we make disastrous choices leading to disease, death, and destruction, as in war, murder, fatal accidents, the death of innocent children, and other human tragedies, daily presented to us in all their distressing details in the media. Julian did not attempt to explain the Black Death, any more than we can explain AIDS. She did insist that such evils would never triumph, but were necessary in a way that God had not revealed to us, that they were part of a "great secret" that would be revealed to us only in the life hereafter. This led her to an ultimate feeling of optimism in which "all shall be well," since, in Julian's terms, what is impossible to us is possible to God. This is reason enough for us all to rejoice, and reason for God, in spite of the sometimes disastrous misuse of our freedom of choice, to still regard humanity as God's crowning achievement.

As Julian pleads with us to not be too hard on ourselves in acknowledgment of our sins, so she also cautions us not to become overwrought with anxiety, which can lead to despair. Thus, while Julian sets us an extremely high standard of personal behavior and discipline, she sees the danger of perfectionism and urges moderation. The moderation she recommends was implicit in the rule of the anchoress that she followed, which, although it seems arduous to the present-day aspirant, avoided the extremes of self-mortifying piety available in the fourteenth century. Julian assures us that the presence of the Holy Spirit in our lives is the certain antidote to our fears and anxieties, the force by which God's saving and healing power is present to us in all we undertake.

Julian identifies, however, both the positive and negative aspects of such fears as may arise in us. What she describes as "holy dread" draws us to God. Naked fear purges us, and despair makes us long for God. Thus a full understanding of God's love for us is possible only as a result of our fears aroused by the potential absence of that love. Love and fear can be seen to be mutually interdependent. Our optimism, and Julian's, is based on the fact that God will not allow our fears to overcome us any more than God will allow sin and evil to triumph in our lives.

17

A Life of Prayer

If the concept of "oneing" may be described as Julian's prime contribution to her potential effect on contemporary theology, it is in the area of prayer that we can identify her greatest contribution in the field of spirituality. In the fourteenth century, Julian called Christians back from an overcomplicated ritual of prayer through a plethora of saints and other intermediaries and suggested that prayer was at its most effective when it was addressed directly to God. If there was to be any intermediary, it was to be Christ.

Julian acknowledged the traditional steps in the mystic's journey from purgation through illumination to union with God, but did not, I believe, follow the classic pattern of viewing this progression in the form of a ladder, or scale, as Walter Hilton insisted. I sense that Julian was, instead, open to the fact that at different times our spiritual journey encounters different moods and that we engage in the spiritual exercise most suited to our mood at a particular time. There are times when we perceive our need to be purged of all that preoccupies us. At other moments we receive insights into our faith, fragments in the illuminative process, new understandings of who we are and what role God plays in our lives, followed by a renewed sense of God's purpose for us. And there are, albeit for most of us only on rare occasions, those times when we feel the close presence of God, when we are at peace with ourselves and the world and able to grasp what Brother Lawrence, a French Carmelite mystic of the seventeenth century, called "the practice of the presence of God." Julian understands that these different spiritual states are not necessarily progressive, and that having moved from one to another, we are not permanently situated in a new elevated state. We are, rather, bound to return to a state in which we encounter further need for purgation and illumination, in preparation for further experiences of union with God, a state that achieves fullness and permanence only in the life hereafter.

Not only does Julian describe what I would define as a circular pattern of spiritual existence, which reflects my own experience, but she encourages us by reminding us that God has historically chosen the most human and least perfect individuals to become the saints of the church, citing as examples, among others, Mary Magdalene, Peter, and Paul. We are reminded that Christ himself told us that he came not to call the righteous, but sinners to repentance. Julian is at heart a realist, and it is this realism that allows us to embark on a renewed life of prayer, recognizing at the outset that we may not achieve the advanced level of spiritual sophistication evident in Julian's own spiritual practice.

As described in my earlier treatment of her theology of prayer, Julian divides prayer into three principal categories: petitionary prayer, contemplative prayer, and prayer of thanksgiving or praise. We need to remember that, for Julian, prayer and life were inseparable. For her, prayer was life and life was prayer. In our prayer, which "oneth the soul to God," we are enjoined to pray boldly, to pray directly to God, and to pray with joy. Julian wants her "even-Christians" to be suffused with joy, a joy that we would do well to recover in both our personal devotions and our public worship. There is nothing grim about Julian's relationship to God. She gains distinct pleasure from her spiritual exercises, a pleasure that can be found only in those who make such exercises part of their daily routine and habit, where familarity breeds not contempt, but the sense of a warm and joyful presence. I believe that much of the discomfort experienced by people today in both their personal prayer life and their presence in corporate worship springs from the lack of this very familarity that Julian's prayer life exudes, an intimacy with God for which we all yearn.

In petitionary prayer, which Julian also calls prayer of "kind yearning" and "beseeching" prayer, we begin by recognizing that it is God who makes us want to pray. Therefore we need not fear that we are not praying correctly or that God is not aware of our efforts, because it is God making us pray, in the way in which we are praying, which is the correct way for us. We need not be bound by any rigid "rules" as we pray, although this freedom does not negate the benefits of having a personal "rule of life" or discipline of prayer. It is also God who makes us ask for our needs, whether those needs are our own or the needs of others for whom we have been asked or for whom we feel the need to pray. In petitionary prayer, Julian also observes, we do indeed ask for our needs, of which God is already aware. The acknowledgment of our needs is therefore an important element of our growth in awareness of how we relate to God. While we may at times feel guilty at presenting God with a long "shopping list" of needs, God uses this form of prayer to strengthen our communication with God and to help us develop a stronger sense of ourselves within the divine plan.

Too often, however, either individually or corporately, we offer our petitionary prayers, handing our concerns over to God, and then wait for God to act while we return to our mundane and hectic secular occupations. An often neglected element of petitionary prayer is that period of silent receptiveness, in which we allow God to answer our prayers. Julian assures us that God will respond, but not always necessarily in the manner we anticipated. It is in acquiring the ability to hear God's responses that we will begin to be transformed and find our lives acquiring a centeredness we had not previously known, for we not only hear God on these occasions, but learn to act on what we hear.

Contemplative prayer was a staple in Julian's spiritual diet and, I believe, is the form of prayer we most need to recover and develop in our spiritual journeys today. In a world that places such a premium on every aspect of control, it is perhaps hard to realize the importance of total surrender to God, a state in which we are seeking and seeing God's presence, utterly removed from the business and preoccupations of this world, gazing upon the person of Christ. There is no formula for this manner of praying, which makes it at one and the same time extraordinarily simple and extraordinarily difficult. Such prayer is simple because it requires no equipment other than ourselves—no books, no costumes, no specific times or spaces, no officials or professionals. It is difficult because it demands that we set ourselves aside from all other company and occupations and devote ourselves literally wholeheartedly to God. This devotion takes constant and continuing practice, acquired through the type of discipline under which Julian placed herself, varying only in the degree to which we are capable of prioritizing our time. The Christian has much to learn from the Eastern religions when it comes to this form of meditative prayer, but we are not on totally foreign ground within the Christian tradition, especially if we return to the Ignatian tradition and understand the journey undertaken by mystics such as Julian in the medieval period.

To begin to achieve a balanced diet in our own prayer lives, it is therefore necessary to allow regular times of silent, contemplative prayer, in addition to the daily discipline achieved by such exercises as the saying of the daily office. Such a balance might be gained by giving silent meditation the same amount of time each day as we allot to our daily office. This may seem a little arduous for those for whom it comes as a new concept, in which case the "equal time" formula could be set as a target to achieve over a period of time.

Prayer of praise and thanksgiving should flow naturally from the other two forms of prayer, as we acknowledge with joy our renewed relationship to God, both in our personal prayer life and in our corporate worship. Even in her darkest moments, Julian is filled with the sense of joy and thanksgiving and recounts the laughter she experienced during her revelations, a laughter in which Christ himself joined. Too often our thanksgiving is perfunctory and dutiful, because we have lost touch with the spontaneous joy to be encountered as we assume a closer relationship to God through Christ. As suggested in my earlier treatment of prayer, and as reiterated in my discussion of the roles of purgation, illumination, and union with God, it is my contention that Julian kept her spiritual life in balance by moving freely from one form of communication with God to another, to include petition, contemplation, thanksgiving, praise and joy, all centered on and surrounded by God's unbounded love, expressed to us in the person of Christ.

Engagement in such a life of prayer can only lead to what can truly be called eternal optimism, an optimism founded on God's promise of eternity for us, a promise based on our justification by faith and not by works, although our works will spring from our faith. Julian encourages us to look ahead to God in Jesus and not backward at our past sins and failures. For God is already at work curing our sinfulness, a process that will be completed as we begin our next life, the ultimate reality of our soulful "substance," in Julian's terms. So we ought continuously to look to Christ Jesus, the source of our own true life, and as we do so, we will begin to experience the true joy of realizing that eventually all shall be well.

Selected Bibliography

R.W. Ackerman and R. Dahood. *Ancrene Riwle: Introduction and Part I*. Medieval and Renaissance Studies. Vol. 31. Binghamton, N.Y.: SUNY, 1984.

R.S. Allen. *Richard Rolle, The English Writings*. New York: Paulist Press, 1991.

C.W. Atkinson. *Mystic and Pilgrim, The Book and The World of Margery Kempe*, Ithaca, N.Y.: Cornell University Press, 1983.

F. Barlow. *The English Church, 1056–1154*. London: Longman, 1979.

F. Beer. *Julian of Norwich's Revelations of Divine Love* (The Shorter Version). Middle English Texts. Heidelberg: Heidelberg University Press, Winter, 1978.

M.M. Blake. *The Glory and the Sorrow of Norwich*. 3d ed. Norwich: Jarrold, ca. 1907.

F. Blomefield. *An Essay Towards a Topographical History of the County of Norfolk*, with a Continuation by the Rev. Charles Parkin. 5 vols. Norwich: Fersfield and Lynn, 1739–1775.

P. Browne. *The History of Norwich*. Norwich: R. Chipperfield, 1814.

C.W. Bynum. *Jesus as Mother: Studies in the Spirituality of the High Middle Ages*. Berkeley: University of California Press, 1982.

G. Chaucer. *The Complete Works: The Riverside Chaucer*. Oxford: Oxford University Press, 1987.

J.P.H. Clark. "The Trinitarian Theology of Walter Hilton's Scale of Perfection, Book Two." In *Langland, the Mystics and the Medieval English Religious Tradition*, ed. H. Phillips. Cambridge: D.S. Brewer, 1990.

J.P.H. Clark and R. Dorward. *Walter Hilton, The Scale of Perfection*. New York: Paulist Press, 1991.

R.M. Clay. *The Hermits and Anchorites of England*. London: Methuen, 1914.

E. Colledge, O.S.A., and J. Walsh, S.J. *A Book of Showings to the Anchoress Julian of Norwich*. 2 vols. Toronto: Pontifical Institute of Mediaeval Studies, 1978.

E. Colledge, O.S.A., and J. Walsh, S.J. *Julian of Norwich, Showings*, New York: Paulist Press, 1978.

E. Colledge, O.S.A. *The Medieval Mystics of England*. London: John Murray, 1961.

N. Davis. *Non-Cycle Plays and Fragments*. London: Early English Text Society, Supplementary Text I, p.xxxv.

J.C. Dickinson. *An Ecclesiastical History of England: The Later Middle Ages*. London: A. & C. Black, 1979.

E.J. Dobson. *The English Text of the Ancrene Riwle, B.M. Cotton MS Cleopatra, C.VI*. Oxford: Early English Text Society, Series no. 267, 1972.

C. Dyer. *Standards of Living in the Later Middle Ages*. Cambridge: Cambridge University Press, 1989.

E. Ennen. *The Medieval Woman*. Oxford: Basil Blackwell, 1989.

B. Ford, ed. "The Age of Chaucer." In *The Pelican Guide to English Literature*. London: Penguin Books, 1954.

S. Fox. *The Medieval Woman*. Boston: Little Brown, 1985.

M. Glasscoe. *Julian of Norwich, A Revelation of Love*. Exeter: Exeter Medieval English Texts and Studies, 1986.

B. Green and R.M.R. Young. *Norwich, the Growth of a City*. Norwich: City of Norwich Museums, 1968.

R. Griffiths. "The Later Middle Ages." In *The Oxford Illustrated History of Britain*. Oxford: Oxford University Press, 1984.

W. Hilton. *The Ladder of Perfection*. London: Penguin Books, 1957.

D.R. Howard. *Chaucer and the Medieval World*. London: Weidenfeld & Nicholson, 1987.

W. Hudson and J. Tingey. *Records of Norwich*, Vol. II, pp. 311–313. Norwich: Jarrold & Sons, 1906–1910.

G. Jantzen. *Julian of Norwich*. London: S.P.C.K., 1987.

John-Julian, O.J.N. *A Lesson of Love: The Revelations of Julian of Norwich*. London: Darton, Longman & Todd, 1988.

E. Kadloubovsky and E.M. Palmer. *Writings from the Philokalia on Prayer of the Heart*. London: Faber and Faber, 1951.

M. Kempe. *The Book of Margery Kempe*. ed. S.B. Meech and H.E. Allen. The Early English Text Society. Oxford: Oxford University Press, 1940.

M. Kempe. *The Book of Margery Kempe*. trans. B.A. Windeatt. London: Penguin Books, 1985.

D. Knowles. *The English Mystical Tradition*. New York: Harper and Brothers, 1961.

H. Küng. *Eternal Life?* trans. E. Quinn. New York: Doubleday, 1984.

M.W. Labarge. *A Small Sound of the Trumpet: Women in Medieval Life*. Boston: Beacon Press, 1986.

W. Langland. *Piers the Ploughman*. London: Penguin Books, 1959.

K. Leech and B. Ward, S.L.G. *Julian Reconsidered*. Oxford: SLG Press, 1988.

R. Llewellyn. *Love Bade Me Welcome*. London: Darton, Longman & Todd, 1985.

R. Llewellyn. *With Pity Not With Blame*. London: Darton, Longman & Todd, 1982.

R. Llewellyn, ed. *Julian, Woman of our Day*. London: Darton, Longman & Todd, 1985.

E. Mason. *The Role of the English Parishioner, 1100–1500*. Journal of Ecclesiastical History 27. Cambridge: Cambridge University Press, 1976.

K.B. McFarlane. *John Wycliffe and the Beginnings of English Nonconformity*. London: English Universities Press, 1952.

M. McKisack. *The Fourteenth Century*. Oxford: Oxford University Press, 1959.

M. McLean. *Who was Julian? A Beginner's Guide*. Norwich: Julian Shrine Publications, 1984.

S.B. Meech and H.E. Allen. *The Book of Margery Kempe*. Early English Text Society. Oxford: Oxford University Press, 1940.

T. Merton. *Conjectures of a Guilty Bystander*. London: Burns and Oates, 1965.

P. Molinari, S.J. *Julian of Norwich: The Teaching of a Fourteenth Century English Mystic*. New York: Longmans Green, 1958.

R.A. Moody. *Life after Life*. St. Simon's Island, Georgia: Mockingbird Books, 1975.

A.R. Myers. *England in the Late Middle Ages*. London: Penguin Books, 1952.

J.H. Parry. *Registrum Johannis de Trillek, episcopi Herefordensis, A.D. MCCCXLIV–MCCCLXI*. Canterbury and York Society, 1912, p. 393.

B. Pelphrey. *Christ Our Mother: Julian of Norwich*. London: Darton, Longman & Todd, 1989.

B. Pelphrey. *Love Was His Meaning, The Theology and Mysticism of Julian of Norwich*. Salzburg: Salzburg Studies in English Literature, 1982.

E.A. Petroff. *Medieval Women's Visionary Literature*. Oxford: Oxford University Press, 1986.

H. Phillips, ed. *Langland, the Mystics and the Medieval English Religious Tradition*, Essays in Honor of S.S. Hussey. Cambridge: D.S. Brewer, 1990.

T. Rowley. *The High Middle Ages*. London: Collins, 1986.

J.K. Ryan. trans. *The Confessions of St. Augustine*. New York: Doubleday, 1960.

M.B. Salu. *The Ancrene Riwle*. London: Burns and Oates, 1955.

A. Savage and N. Watson. *Anchoritic Spirituality, Ancrene Wisse and Associated Works*. New York: Paulist Press, 1991.

F.D. Sayer, ed. *Julian and Her Norwich*. Norwich: Julian of Norwich 1973 Celebration Committee, 1973.

L. Shirley-Price and C. Wolters. *Walter Hilton: The Ladder of Perfection*. London: Penguin Books, 1988.

M. Smith. *Pre-Reformation England*. London: Macmillan, 1938.

R.N. Swanson. *Church and Society in Late Medieval England*. Oxford: B. Blackwell, 1989.

N. Tanner. *The Church in Late Medieval Norwich, 1370–1532*. Toronto: Pontifical Institute of Mediaeval Studies, 1984.

J.A. Thompson. *The Transformation of Medieval England, 1370–1529*. London: Longmans, 1983.

R.H. Thouless. *The Lady Julian: A Psychological Study*. London: S.P.C.K, 1924.

E. Underhill. *Mysticism*. New York: E.P. Dutton, 1930.

E. Underhill. *Mystics of the Church*. Harrisburg, PA: Morehouse, 1988.

R. Virgoe, ed. *Private Life in the Fifteenth Century*. London: Weidenfeld & Nicholson, 1989.

J.J. Walsh, S.J. *The Revelations of Divine Love of Julian of Norwich*. Wheathamstead: Anthony Clarke Books, 1961.

J.J. Walsh, S.J. *The Cloud of Unknowing*. New York: Paulist Press, 1981.

B.A. Windeatt. *The Book of Margery Kempe*. London: Penguin Books, 1985.

C. Wolters. *Julian of Norwich: Revelations of Divine Love*. London: Penguin Books, 1966.

P. Ziegler. *The Black Death*. London: Penguin Books, 1969.

86644